A Blessed Life

Benedictine Guidelines for Those Who Long
for Good Days

Wil Derkse

Translated by Martin Kessler

LITURGICAL PRESS
Collegeville, Minnesota

www.litpress.org

Cover design by David Manahan, OSB. Contemporary icon of Saint Benedict by Mary Charles McGough, OSB. Courtesy of Saint Scholastica Monastery, Duluth, Minnesota.

This book was originally published in Dutch under the title *Gezegend leven: Benedictijnse richtlijnen voor wie naar goede dagen verlangt* © Uitgeverij Lannoo nv, Tielt, 2007, The Netherlands. All rights reserved.

Scripture texts in this work are taken from the *New Revised Standard Version Bible* © 1989, Division of Christian Education of the National Council of the Churches of Christ in the United States of America. Used by permission. All rights reserved.

1	2	3	4	5	6	7	8

Library of Congress Cataloging-in-Publication Data

Derkse, Wil.
    [Gezegend leven. English]
    A blessed life : Benedictine guidelines for those who long for good days / Wil Derkse ; translated by Martin Kessler.
        p.   cm.
    Includes bibliographical references.
    ISBN 978-0-8146-1863-9
    1. Benedict, Saint, Abbot of Monte Cassino. Regula.   2. Spiritual life—Christianity.   I. Title.

BX3004.Z5D4613 2009
255'.106—dc22

2008022000

For
Anne, fellow founder of our little community,
Godelieve, with whom I enjoy praying in the crypt of the
house that Anselm helped to build,
Andrea, the prioress who corrects me as a sister,
and *Gibert*, the cellarer who tackles everything.

Contents

Introduction

Who does not long for good days, for a life on which blessing rests? In the Prologue of his Rule for monks, St. Benedict invites his readers and potential followers to join him and in that invitation he cites John's gospel and Psalm 34: "And what does He say: 'Come, my sons, listen to me: I will teach you the fear of the Lord. Hasten, as long as you have life, so that the darkness of death may not overcome you.' While the Lord, in the midst of all those people whom he calls, seeks for laborers, he repeats: 'Who is the man, who longs for life and wishes to see good days?' When you hear this and answer: 'I,' then God says to you . . ." (RB Prol. 112-16).[1]

While this language may sound rather archaic, two things are clear at once. Benedict's program is fully dynamic: we need to hurry to give a good turn to our life. For the rest, it will subsequently appear that we, having made that choice, still have a long and patient way to go. The second element is that Benedict offers a way of life which grants joy and contentment, a life on which blessing rests. Who does not long for "good days"? The Benedictine perspective wants to be attractive, as we will read further on in the Prologue. That does not mean that this way is easy, but that is true of everything worthwhile. How much practice is needed before anyone can play the cello concert of Edward Elgar superbly? Anyone who begins this way is often attracted by something or more often, by someone: an experience of a concert, or the film about the cellist Jacqueline du Pré, or a teacher. It costs a lot of effort and much guidance by experienced musicians to develop into a cellist who in turn knows how to touch the souls of others. But what gratification and joy when the music really succeeds! At that point, the patient drudgery and persistent practice is forgotten.

Benedict presents to his candidates a comparable road:

> We will therefore establish a training school for the service of the Lord. In its plan we hope to prescribe nothing that is too difficult, or that is too heavy. If something should occur in it which seems quite severe, but is required on reasonable grounds for the improvement of mistakes and maintaining love, do not be frightened instantly and do not flee from the way of salvation, which is always narrow at the outset. (RB Prol. 45-48)

The (excellent) translator is here a bit "severe"; the Latin text is milder: "Too," which is used twice in the translation, "too difficult," "too heavy" does not occur in the Latin text, but perhaps the translator, Father Frans Vromen, wished to make a small correction of Benedict on the basis of his ample monastic experience. It would be unrealistic that in the monastic way of life (as in all other ways of life), the difficult and hard parts would be lacking. An experienced monk, who apparently experienced a difficult period in his life in the monastic community, once said about the vow of *stabilitas* (the persistent "sticking with it"): "For me, *stabilitas* means that I say to myself in the morning while I am shaving: I am not yet leaving today."

But we are dealing here with an inviting Prologue, sketching an attractive picture. That also is suggested by the expression "rather hard"—the Latin text has *paululum restrictius*. The dictionary has for *paululus* "rather minor," "a little," "a touch," meanings that do not inspire fear but do indicate that discipline and perseverance will be needed. A monastery is not a spiritual massage parlor. But the practicing of the right attitudes is worthwhile and the road becomes easier and more joyful because of the progress one makes: "As one makes progress in the monastic life and in faith, however, the heart is enlarged as one rushes along the way of God's commandments with unspeakable joyous love" (RB Prol. 49-50).

Monastic life, according to the Trappist Michael Casey, is the absolute opposite of an aimless life. It has a goal and it has developed a tested and well-regulated network of means by which that goal may be realized.[2]

The rhythm and the progress of monastic life are directed toward optimally setting people on the road toward joy for which they are destined.

With those who are presently the eldest in the abbey to which I am attached, I note in all sorts of little things that they are such vital people internally. Sometimes we jokingly (but also lovingly) call these two brothers, who are approaching ninety "our stick brigade." They are mild, ripe, tolerant, and humorous men, not ascetic, dried-out sourpusses. One can hear that in their voices when they read or explain the Scriptures, which they still do regularly. Both have and cultivate their own interests, are faithful participants in the Holy Office and know, through reading, study and the internet, what is going on in our culture. For those in their thirties and forties which we have had among us, and also for us oblates, this is a hopeful sign: Benedictine life, by which one can keep growing, is possible, verse 50 of the Prologue is more than a commercial. To cite a recent book title, spirituality is *a slow-release miracle*.[3]

The lengthy chapter 7, about humility, is at first sight difficult to accept for modern readers, but it closes with a joyful perspective:

> As soon as the monk has climbed all these steps of humility, he will reach the love of God, which is perfect and excludes fear. Through this love he will accomplish everything which he formerly completed with a certain anxiety, as if he did it habitually or out of a natural impulse. He no longer acts out of anxiety of hell but out of the love of Christ and is driven by the habit itself to do good and by the joy he finds in virtue. (RB 7.67-69)

Benedict here joins the classical thought that virtue is not decency but *excellence*, a gradually trained and acquired habit—directed to the good—to offer "quality," an activity that brings joy with it, as when an excellent cellist brings her public and herself an unforgettable evening.

The Benedictine program is indeed directed toward "good days" and toward joy. A monastic community is not intended to be a sour and joyless prison.

I am therefore always disturbed when someone, for example, a well-meaning Dutch television personality such as Leo Fijen, though an admirable champion of monastic life, in an (otherwise inspiring) documentary on *Le Grande Chartreuse* keeps talking about the "severest monastery in the world," as if a group of masochists were living there together. As in a discussion of the film *Into Great Silence* by one of our better columnists, Marjoleine de Vos, in which a certain affinity for the monastic life is conveyed, I also read sentences with phrases like "they must there . . . ;" "they are not allowed to . . ." and "they would never . . . ," which almost make one forget that the brothers *enjoy* being there. Certainly, the followers of Saint Bruno have a rougher lifestyle than the daughters and sons of Saint Benedict, but this is about a personally chosen roughness, which moreover can be accommodated (it seems that the superior often wants to accommodate, but the community does not, or only hesitatingly) and that it moreover may be arranged differently on the local level. The Carthusians of Parkminster near London—but that is a *British* Carthusian monastery—have arranged their house more tastefully and in all austerity have appointed things somewhat "more pleasant" than their more rugged fellow brothers in the mountains near Grenoble (France).

No matter how it is arranged, monastic life is not intended to be an ascetic prison where people may be kept small and curtailed, but a place to grow, as a person and as a community. It is remarkable that this lifestyle has remained vital for about 1500 years, though, of course, there have been historically and locally worrisome periods and they will also occur in the future. Also, the monastic life keeps attracting people, in many forms and in varying ways of bonding. More and more people who do not wish to be or cannot be religious, find nurturing ideals and attitudes which they can allow to be fruitful in their own context of life.

In a previous book, which aimed at an introductory "translation" of the Benedictine spirituality toward non-monastic contexts, I discussed a few central Benedictine ideals and attitudes.[4] Some of the central themes are: the cultivation of the art of attentive listening (*auscultare*) and answering from the heart, the vows of stability, the change of the organization of life and obedience, the lessons of Benedict about providing fruitful leadership and bearing responsibility, the Benedictine dealing with time. The book drew, and still draws, many readers and it is understandable that relatively soon my friendly publisher carefully asked whether a sequel was forthcoming. That was not my original plan. The Rule of Benedict is only a thin book without a sequel. I thought I might follow the same pattern.

Benedict himself calls his Rule a "rule for beginners." He did not write a "rule for the advanced," though he does give some advice on reading that might take people further. Also, experts have observed that his Rule, as it has come to us, may have been augmented by himself of a second, additional part. The first part closes with the little chapter on porters of the monastery. At the gate we reach the boundary of the monastery. That is where the reach of the Rule really ends. Since the monastery is supposed to be self-supporting, we read in the penultimate verse, monks do not need to go past the gate, for "that is definitely not good for their souls." Then follows the closing verse: "We desire that this Rule will often be read to the congregation, so that not a single brother can pretend ignorance as an excuse" (RB 66.8). This suggests that Benedict is finished. However, in the final version another seven chapters follow, about matters which he had not thought about (chapter 67 is about "the brothers who have been sent on a journey"), about nuancing the previous, and about matters that in their community apparently caused problems, followed by some advices for further reading.

That I yet wrote a sequel to my previous book has, I realize, related causes. I have also kept reading texts of contemporary (and earlier) mothers and fathers who have provided commentary for the Benedictine tradition, and have thought it through, such as Joan Chittister, Michaela Puzicha, Aquinata Böckman, Anselm Grün, Aelred of Rievaulx, Michael Casey, Leo Fijen, Christopher Jamison, Benet Tvedten, and certainly many others. Where possible, in future chapters I shall mention my sources somewhat more precisely, but often this is about gradual reading, which trickled into my mind and became more or less appropriated thoughts, than about the fruit of systematic, scholarly study.

Additionally, after the publication of the book I had the opportunity to discuss it with many people. This meant that I needed to supplement and nuance subjects on which I had written and that I could augment certain themes with interesting new possibilities for application. I am most grateful that I was able to learn from so many at this time. This process also led to some essays and chapters in books, which have received a place in adapted and expanded form in what follows. Some overlapping and repetition may have taken place, but that is also the case in the Rule—and Benedict probably knew the ancient saying *repetitio est mater studiorum*.

Because I cannot assume that everyone who will read this book has read the previous book, the opening chapter offers a summarizing first introduction of the important aspects of Benedictine spirituality.

Thereafter follow some additional Benedictine attitudes that may also be fruitful in non-monastic contexts. When I put them together, I noted that it is always about attitudes and virtues that both contrast with traits of character of contemporary culture and yet are painfully missed in our culture.

1. The cultivation of a climate of silence and rest. In a culture of continuous and often loud background noise and an abundance of external stimuli it might be sensible to develop and maintain structural situations of "back-

ground silence" in which we might be attentive to that which merits our attention.

2. The serious (but relaxed) dedication to daily work and to daily study. In a culture where the pressure of work is considerable for many and work is at the same time (partly) seen as a necessary evil—we live toward weekends, vacations, and retirement—Benedict teaches us that daily work is a "necessary good," in which and to which we can grow spiritually, may be creative and contribute to the flourishing of person and community. In a culture of rapid, but only superficial streams of information, a daily portion of solid reading (in a monastic community it is obligatory for everyone, not only for intellectuals) might contribute to one's own soul and the soul of others remaining fresh, open, and alive.

3. The appropriation of the virtue of humility—etymologically "the courage to serve." In a culture of exaggeration, window-dressing behavior, ambition, priority lists, gaudy things, and unjustified bonuses, Benedict teaches us the realistic human image that all of us are but fragile, limited little beings, but with the capacity to grow. Such growth is done optimally by "service," in which we highly esteem others and other things.

4. The mutually related virtues of hospitality, care, good and fruitful stewardship, respect, gentleness, quiet patience, intelligent capacity to discern, and "generativity" (by which one generation helps another grow toward fruitful independence), which contrasts strongly with a culture of isolation, laxity, sloppy waste, cynicism, coarseness, and the quick gleaning of "competences" in instrumental contexts of learning.

5. Benedict stresses the importance of discipline, correction of what is wrong, and frugality—but also the importance of festive and joyful celebration: contrasting anew with

a culture of indifferent tolerance, overconsumption, and unlimited superficial pleasure. He suggests positive ways to arrive at "durable" joy.

6. For a good personal and social life, Benedict stresses repeatedly the crucial importance of listening attentively and from the heart, and of speaking of "good words," said and used in the right manner. In a culture of rapid worldwide communication, "speaking evil" (*maledicere*) sometimes leads to quickly branching out cascades of evil and violence. However, the opposite (*benedicere*) leads many to a blessed life and good days.

All these attitudes may be cultivated outside of the monastery walls—they may be practiced also outside of the "school for the Lord." They are realistic guidelines for a personally and socially blessed and fruitful life. Andrew Nugent claims that the Benedictine movement possesses a strong restorative potential, which may bring health, intelligence, and wisdom in a culture of fragmentation and aimlessness.

In a summarizing conversation at the end of a seminar on these themes, the participants remarked many times that what Benedict teaches is so commonsensical and concretely doable: "I can just start with this tomorrow." Such a beginning is not so difficult—as always, persistence is something else again. This is of course regularly and with good reason pointed out to the author of these lines by those most near to him. To these beloved ones this little book is dedicated.

1

Benedictine Life:
Vital and Attractive

One of my students in religious studies told me enthusiastically in a break between classes about a fine vacation she had spent in a pleasant hotel on the shore near the Benedictine abbey of Maria Laach. She was surprised to hear that I had written my Nijmegen University oration there in 2002. She was still more surprised when I told her that I am associated as an oblate with the Saint Willibrord's Abbey in Doetinchem.[5] "Are there then abbeys in the Netherlands also?" she asked in amazement. I pointed out to her the website www.monasteria.org, on which are presented the more than forty monasteries of the Benedictine family (male and female Benedictines, Cistercians, male and female Trappists) in the Low Countries.

I often get such a reaction, as do my fellow oblates (more than sixty) and fellow brothers (eight presently live in our abbey). Monastic life is seen as a museological affair and a rapidly disappearing heritage, if it has not already disappeared.

But monastic life remains stubbornly vital. The fifteen-hundred-year-old Rule of Benedict is used worldwide by tens of thousands of monks and nuns as a guide for their life together. Almost as many and an increasing number of men and women who live outside the monastery have associated themselves as oblate or associate members, with the Rule playing a role in their own conduct of life. This is not about copying the monastic life but about appropriating it for themselves in a suitable form.

There is, of course, talk about increasing attention for monastic spirituality and life. It attracts people, sometimes quite literally. On the open Monastery Day 2006, our little abbey had more than 2,500 people visiting. Maria Laach, a monastic magnet on a beautiful lake in the German Eifel, draws annually more than a million visitors. Some come only for the delicious natural products in the monastery store and the beautiful art gallery, but almost all at least briefly walk into the well maintained medieval church. At the Divine Offices there are always a lot of people.

That even a brief contact with monastic spirituality may touch people, I saw happen in a group of twenty-four students with whom I stayed for a weekend in Saint Willibrord's Abbey. That visit was part of an academic course on religious experience, with lectures by a brain specialist, a psychologist of religion, an expert on spirituality, and an eminent mathematician who also teaches Buddhist meditation. I was giving an introduction to Benedictine spirituality and I accompanied the group with a few other teachers into the abbey. Because it was about "experience," the students were invited to experience the entire monastic rhythm: the five daily Divine Offices (the first at 6:15 a.m.), (Zen) meditation, celebration of the Eucharist, close reading of a mystical text by Ruysbroeck, led by the then eighty-five-year-old Father Gerard Helwig, common meals, recreation, study sessions, and to bed on time. Of the twenty-four students, four were "active" in church (choir member, lector, assistant at Mass); the others were rather "something–sometime" believers in that they now and then attended church at family events.

Their "just going along" had an impact on all of them. At the first celebration, the Vespers on Friday afternoon, some students sang along. More than ten celebrations later, on Sunday afternoon, all of them sang and jumped up at each penultimate psalm verse so they could bow at the "Glory to the Father, the Son and the Holy Spirit . . ." Outside and in the corridors of the guest rooms, I heard much humming. With all of them something happened. In an evaluating conversation a few weeks later, all the students, without exception, found this the high point of their study year. They decided to write letters to the brothers about their experiences; I put copies in the monastic library. One of the students wrote that when she came home, she immediately straightened out her very cluttered room. She had lived for a few days in a beautiful, orderly environment and saw the contrast with what she encountered at home. Monastic cleanliness, according to Dom Denis Huerre, who was abbot of the beautiful abbey *La Pierre-qui-vire*, is not a luxury but a necessity, which is the more respected as people see a divine task in this.

Another student found it to be a tiring weekend, with a full daily order, but she was very grateful for it, for she had rediscovered that she could sing and so she had signed up with a chamber chorus. Thus, no monastic entries, but a response to the experience that one can live (a little) differently. The monastic life offers room and hospitality for many. The "search after God," which is cultivated there, is open and in a sense "supra-confessional."

People appear to become increasingly sensitive to this. The cloister series that Leo Fijen produced for KRO/RKK (Dutch Catholic Radio and Television) drew many viewers. More than three million in Great Britain viewed the series *The Monastery* and *The Convent*, about men and women who lived with Benedictines and Poor Clares. The books by Anselm Grün and other monastic authors are read worldwide by a comparable number of people.

Moreover, more and more people choose to continue beyond the nurture of an uncommitted longing and join as an oblate, after a preparatory year, or (in the monasteries of the Cistercian family) as an associated member. Our own group of oblates, for example, has doubled in numbers in a decade. The left-liberal weekly *Vrij Nederland* in January 2006 dedicated a detailed and serious report on this "Benedictine life beyond the monastic walls."

But, of course, it would not work without living communities of monks and nuns where we and other guests can regularly "log in." However, I am not overly concerned about that. Some communities merge or move to a home for the elderly; others invest in new and large guest houses and experience growth. And even at a great age, one may still be vital, as I wrote about our two elderly folk in the introduction of this book.

The actual situation of monastic life does not look moribund worldwide. More than one thousand three hundred communities with approximately thirty-five thousand monks and nuns, as well as tens of thousands of oblates related to these communities, live according to the almost fifteen-hundred-year-old Rule of Benedict. Apparently the Rule has sufficient suppleness and flexibility to also "regulate" living and working together of religious in the twenty-first century.

This worldwide network of monastic life moves daily, as it were, a wave of songs of praise across the earth. When in our own area the monks and nuns close the day with the singing of the so-called Compline, they sing in Saint John's Abbey in Minnesota approximately Sext (the sung afternoon prayer); and in Vietnam (with seven priories), the monks and nuns begin their day with Lauds.

This worldwide monastic network is quite easy to visit at present. Via www.osb.org, a general Benedictine website based in Saint John's Abbey, many websites may be found of communities of male and female Benedictines, male and female Cistercians, male and female Trappists, who offer virtual hospitality via the internet. These websites are visited by many people. There are daily tens of thousands of hits of visitors worldwide who are led by an abbey, download the last sermon of the abbot, listen to the sung prayer of the Divine Office, order spiritual literature, and ask information concerning the possibility of lodging in the guesthouse. Those guesthouses, also those in the Netherlands and Flanders, should better be booked long in advance.

Thus, not a moribund rest and a collection of cultural-historically valuable ruins, but a living and growing network of monastic life.

The purely "being there" of the monastic life, the fact that it is there and is alive, is already a sign with meaning for our time. It is a spirituality of the presence. The actor Alec Guiness writes about his stay in an English Trappist abbey where he had the feeling that he might look inside one of the "spiritual turbines" that keep this world going. It is, of course, important to know what monastic life offers in content. It appeals to the spiritual longing in our time (and at any time) and offers to that longing tested, non-esoteric models of response and growth.

This concept of "spirituality" appears not only somewhat fashionable—"Please do something in your lecture with spirituality"; this is how I was once invited by telephone—but also vague and free-floating. While it is about a longing to keep alive as a human, spirituality has to do with the zest of life, life orientation, lifestyle, and change of life. In many religions and cults, cadres have been developed to give a foundation to this human longing for spiritual life. Benedictine spirituality is one among many, but with ancient testimonials and a remarkable vitality.

Order with Flexibility

Benedict wrote his Rule for the third community he led, that of Monte Cassino, and possibly also for some neighboring communities. By then, he had already some thirty years of monastic experience, with probably quite a few ups and downs. Monastic rules already existed before, for example, those of Augustine—also such a vital document, as the members of the Augustinian family and the Norbertines can testify. Benedict has borrowed much from an unknown master, whose Rule is called the *Regula Magistri*. Some sections he has copied literally. But where he deviates from the text, he is milder in his changes and additions; he is more nuanced and more realistic when the subject is the tasks entrusted to the brothers when they may be doable or when they may be impossible for them to accomplish. Perhaps he had been too severe and too demanding in his earlier periods as spiritual leader with responsibility. This severity is not lacking in his Rule, but it is a milder severity or sometimes rather a severe mildness. Particularly in his "own" chapters he shows himself to be sensitive to the differences between people and to the concern to have respect for such differences. The prudent moderation that characterizes his Rule applies also to the giving of rules itself and to the maintenance of such rules.

Two of many examples of this attitude are the little chapter on the measure of the wine and the chapters on the division of the psalms among the daily prayer Offices.

How much wine may a (South Italian) monk use, as far as Benedict is concerned? First, he remarks that he determines the portions for others with some hesitation, because people do differ. He also claims that the weakness of the less strong needs to be taken into account. Additionally, he proposes a measure of (what has been estimated) a quarter or perhaps half of a liter per person per day. But he nuances his proposal immediately for "when the local circumstances of the work or the summer heat require a greater quantity, then the superior must judge," with, of course, a warning against excess. Rules and their application must be seen in their contexts, as also appears from the conclusion of this little chapter: "Where by local circumstances the above named quantity is not available, but much less or nothing at all, the residents praise God without complaint."

There is a second example of this joining of order with flexibility. The Rule contains a series of chapters in which Benedict divides the one hundred fifty psalms in great detail among the prayer Offices, with directions for their sequence, the nature of the readings, deviations with Sundays or feast days, etc. This continues for many pages, but at the end of this detailed summation there appears an almost humorous note: "We wish to underscore particularly that whoever finds this division of psalms less successful, let him invent another order if he knows a better one." Provided this occurs in an orderly fashion and all psalms receive a turn.

With the concrete translation of these and other proposals of Benedict, the concern is to reckon in an intelligent way with the context in which a monastic congregation is founded, with the nature and composition of that community, and with the living nature of the basic traits that must be maintained and the lines of force of Benedictine spirituality. That explains the multiformity in which Benedictine life shows itself. At Monte Cassino, some wine is on the table in the afternoon; in Saint Willibrord's Abbey there is water (unless it is an important feast day). In the abbey of Saint Benedictusberg at Vaals, to which no school or other activity is related, and that would demand the daily care of a goodly number of monks, six prayer Offices are sung; at Saint John's Abbey, three. But that surely does not mean that in Minnesota there are only watered-down Benedictines: it is a true, powerful center of well-cared-for liturgy, prayer, and study, of which the fruits radiate worldwide through their publishing house, Liturgical Press.

The Rule of Benedict is not a boarded-up canon, says the Trappist Michael Casey. After all, a canon is fixed and static, while the Rule offers structure, but particularly movement and dynamic direction. The Rule is not "complete," neither is the tested monastic life. In the "Council of the Brothers" (RB 3), the younger ones expressly play a role, even an important one. The Spirit "often" offers, Benedict says, a fresh contribution through them. For Michael Casey RB 61.4 is the favorite verse about being open to refreshing influences from an unexpected source. When a visiting monk from "distant places" is a guest, he needs first to accept what he finds. "But if he disapproves something in a reasonable manner and with humble love, or makes a comment, the abbot needs to examine wisely whether the Lord has not sent him precisely with this goal."

Precisely this coming together of order with flexibility makes Benedictine spirituality a living tradition. With the concept of "tradition" we often think of something being static. But the Latin *tradere* indicates a dynamic activity, as we still recognize in the English word *trade*. A living tradition is like a river. Just like a river, a tradition has sources: people, Scripture texts, handed-on rituals. Sources are mostly plural. That is also true of Benedictine life.

To remain fresh and lively, a tradition must remain in contact with its sources, otherwise it dries up. In the Benedictine family, precisely in the past half century, a great deal of work has been done to renew contact with these sources and subsequently to cultivate our Rule and its sources, with early church fathers and pre-Benedictine monastic life in Egypt and Syria, with Celtic monastic culture, together with the reforming contribution of Bernard, with the enriching and fertile treasures of Hildegard of Bingen (Germany), and with the mystic monks. The river of a tradition also knows auxiliary streams: a mental legacy and cultic elements from other cultures. In quite a few monasteries monks and nuns open themselves to God's Word by Zen exercises and silent meditation. With the spiritual guidance in monasteries, grateful use is made from insights of modern human psychology. In African abbeys, for example, dance and rhythm play a more important role in the liturgy than in Sweden.

Just like a river, a tradition has a bed—its form and shape. These are not static, however. A bed can replace itself and change its form. The abbey that I am associated with used to provide its own support, among other things, by maintaining a large, cattle-breeding business. For logistic and personal reasons, it has closed. Presently, a monastic silence and conference center have been established there, with one of the younger monks in charge. It is directed to groups who wish to meet together in the orderly context of monastic life. Again we see here a joining of flexibility concerning the filling in of the work of the monks with order: the continuity of the Benedictine lifestyle, which may also be for non-monastic people a source of *élan*, orientation, and direction for life.

A Few Characteristic Features of Benedictine Spirituality

Benedict was well trained in rhetoric and thus had learned to mind his words. The first word of his Rule is also the most important word. The first sentence is thus the most importance sentence; it contains in a nutshell all the Benedictine life program:

> *Listen, my son, to the guidance of your master, and incline the ear of your heart: accept willingly the admonitions of your loving father and execute them actively.*

Listen! In Latin: *Ausculta*. The verb is a very attentive kind of listening, directed to a fitting reaction. A physician "listens" to his patient with a stethoscope. Not out of curiosity or as a pastime but to listen purposefully to what is going on inside the patient and indeed, that he may judge based on what he has heard to take action or not: to prescribe medication, to consult a specialist, or to organize further clinical study. The goal of Benedictine listening is to learn what a situation demands of you and then to give an appropriate and adequate response. And indeed, as the first sentence says, inclined from the heart to such action. That "inclining" (*inclina*, the imperative of *inclinare*) is to associate with someone, bowing to someone, who is asking something from you: a superior, a brother, a guest, a patient, a colleague, a pupil, a situation, an entire class or division. This is not so much about a question of information, but because an appeal has been made to you, a plea. That first sentence is about saying "yes" from the heart when you have been appealed to. An experienced abbot told me once that it was his habit, when he noted only a slight internal resistance when he laid a demanding task on someone ("Do you wish to be trained to become our new cantor?"), he would say to that person: "Better not do it yet." If someone should begin such a project while his heart is not in it, he is not yet ready for it. If he is genuinely ready for it, the first sentence of the Benedictine Rule executes the movement as it were in one smooth action: be ready to listen and prick up your ears to say "yes" from the heart to what is asked of you, to give an adequate and active response.

Of course, this attitude may also be cultivated outside the monastery. A fellow oblate, who was appointed a school director, withdrew to the abbey before the new school year to prepare

himself for his new task. He wished to translate his bond with
Benedictine spirituality into the context of his work. Quickly, he
concentrated on the first word of the Rule: he earnestly decided
to be a "listening" leader in his school, to give leadership with a
"stethoscope" on.

That is a beautiful goal, but how do you carry it out? In his
case, among other things, by simply being one of the first people
to be in school, and during the tea and coffee hour for new colleagues, to prick up his ears to listen to what was going on and
what was brought up. Not as a self-appointed spy, but to be alert
to small signals to which he might respond heartily and actively.
To continue the stethoscope metaphor: when a little beep is
heard, it might perhaps be prudent to meet separately with the
teacher in the next period, to see whether something might be
done about this small problem together. Because if you do not
react promptly the little "beep" will become a dry cough. If you
wait even longer, the colleague will be home for a few months.

The "listening" coffee hour, however, is not only targeted on
small signals of worries, problems, and strife but also on small
longings and signals of opportunities for growth. Here also one
needs to be alert and to genuinely look for a concrete response: to
see whether the budget permits a new DVD player, pointing to a
course, stimulating a teacher who very much enjoys studying to
tackle a new subject. In the Rule of Benedict the *ausculta* (as does
everything in that Rule, however), pertains also to the abbot. One
of the Rule's pieces of advice for wholesome "abbot's management"
is therefore that he needs to regulate everything with much sense of
rhythm and discretion so that "the weak brothers do not flinch from
what is too difficult for them," but also "that something remains
for the strong to reach toward."

The Three Monastic Vows:
Stability, Change of Lifestyle, Obedience

As in every living and fruitful spirituality, in the first sentence
of the Rule of Benedict the vertical and the horizontal come

together. The alert openness to the word that comes "from on high,"—which might very well come out of the mouth of another person, but in any case from another person whom you want to look up to—must be related to the giving of a response, concretely and actively.

In the three monastic vows, the vertical and the horizontal come together: to *seek for* God in a community and to *follow* Christ (the words "seeking" and "following" are italicized to underscore the dynamics of monastic life. This is different from what an outsider perhaps might think about living in an abbey, that no persons had definitely *found* God and Christ). To live with such a perspective, persistence is needed, with improvement and alert listening in everyday life. That is what the three vows of *stabilitas*, *conversio morum*, and *obedientia* aim at.

Stabilitas refers to saying yes persistently, even when it becomes somewhat more difficult. Negatively put, *stabilitas* is the art of not walking away from those vows and from what you say you have committed yourself to. There are indeed many subtler ways of walking away than only physically leaving a place. *Stabilitas* is persevering in the intention to bloom where you have been planted, and nowhere else, which the dynamics of life does not exclude by any means. Formulated positively, *stabilitas* is persevering in the intention "to stick with it," genuinely to stand ready for what is asked of you here and now. Stability is not an arid immovability to keep standing while you are fully in motion, as a trained surfer.

Conversio morum (in different manuscripts we read the related *conversatio*) may be translated as "change of lifestyle," or gradual growth into the monastic lifestyle. With *conversio* as repentance we quickly think of the radical experiences that may turn life upside down, but that is not intended in *conversio morum*. Rather, it refers to the persistent, daily search for possibilities that might be labeled a "micro-turnabout": answering the telephone a little less grimly, being a bit more courteous and understanding toward your fellow brother who keeps making mistakes in his singing, reading two beautiful poems before going to sleep instead of surfing all the television channels once more. A brother who had worked in the United States for a long time once described *conversio morum* as the daily cleaning up of some *trash* in your life and at the same time concerning yourself with what your *treasures* are.

Obedientia, or obedience, has to do with the *ausculta* of the first sentence of the Rule. The word is derived from *ob-audire*, which means "listening very carefully." This is related to a wider field than obedience in a narrower sense, the following of what your "superior" asks of you, unless you take the concept of "superior" in a wider sense: a professor may view his student as his "superior," or a mother her daughter. Obedience has to do with hearing one another, alert and affectionate listening to what is being asked of you. If one reviews the day from this perspective before going to sleep and asks: was I obedient today?—he will not ask whether he followed the instructions of his superior, but rather: Did I truly listen to the hidden question of that student? Did I put my heart into my reaction? Did I truly respond?

It will be clear that the three perspectives of the quality of *stabilitas, conversio morum*, and *obedientia* are profoundly related and presuppose one another. In the following chapters this triplet of basic attitudes will return regularly and be explored in depth. Hopefully, it will be clear that these attitudes also may be fruitful in other contexts of life than the monastic.

Benedictine Spirituality:
No Frills but a Leaven in *Everything*

The same is true of another basic characteristic of Benedictine spirituality: "that God may be glorified in everything"—*ut in omnibus glorificetur Deus*. The monk does not need to ask which areas are eligible for the praise of God (for example, the prayer of the liturgical Hours) and which are not (for example, peeling potatoes in the kitchen). No choice needs to be made at all: *all* areas offer opportunities to glorify God, and *always*. It is a task that is as simple as it is difficult. It may be noted that this Benedictine motto is found in a very mundane context (quoted from the First Letter of Peter), namely when it relates to the price of the products of work of a monastery: "With the determining of the price the vice of greed may not steal in, but one needs to offer everything a bit cheaper than others can do it 'in the world,' "that God may be glorified in everything." The context of buying and selling is one that may be sanctified—or desecrated. To use modern management jargon, Benedict pleads for *total quality management*, whereby quality is seen in connection with our task to be fellow creator with the Source and the Goal of everything. "He saw that everything was very good."

That the most common, everyday contexts may be served by this Benedictine approach is emphasized by Benedict in the chapter about the one who bears the delegated responsibility for the material management of the monastery, the cellarer (*cellarius*) or steward: "He must view all of the utensils and possessions of the monastery as vessels dedicated to the altar service. He may not neglect anything." Or, if we may put it a bit less dignified way, dishwashing brushes deserve as much respect as do chalices. Everything may be of sacramental value, just as the most common things may be desacralized. Sloppy potato peals with much junk and loss is *zund*, as the people of Brabant say (like the Dutch *zonde*, [sin]).

With this attitude belongs also a careful organization of space and time. Monasteries and their environment often breathe a kind of beauty that is not showy, things are tidied up and in order. Anyone who spends a little time there often longs to straighten out one's own place when returning home, as happened to one of my students. Further, the day is divided in an orderly manner: an order of the day that keeps in mind the hours of the day and our longing to breathe in and out, for relaxation and rest, being alone and in each other's company. The monastic bell that regulates these hours might also chime elsewhere, so that we are stimulated to exercise more in the art of truly beginning, the art of truly quitting, and the art of cultivating both a worthy and a relaxed attitude in our dedication to the task that is acquitted between beginning and ending and that here and now lies before us.

Thus, there are more aspects of Benedictine life that may be fruitfully translated to non-monastic contexts and that may be inspiring for a well-regulated living and working together. In this summarizing sketch, two more points may suffice: Benedictine leadership and dealing with the most serious sin in a monastery, namely, grumbling.

The chapters on the abbot and the cellarer (the steward, or the "head of housekeeping") deserve to be thoroughly considered by anyone who bears extra responsibility. The abbot must be an example of both order and flexibility. Contrary to what the saying "same monks, same hoods" implies, he needs to treat all his fellow brothers differently: "One he must treat with mild goodness, another with reprimands, yet another with the power of persuasion, and thereby accommodate himself according to everyone's nature and capacity of understanding, and thus adapt himself to him, that he not hurt the flock entrusted to him, but rather may rejoice in the growth of a good flock." In other words, lack of flexibility and adaptation is harmful; it is the one who leads who can best adapt himself (and therefore not the inferior), and giving leadership needs to be directed to growth and quality. As in the opening sentence of the Rule, he who bears the greatest responsibility needs to give the best concrete response and needs to have the greatest talent of listening and the greatest talent to incline the ear of the heart—a flexibility that, however, does not at all exclude firmness.

In Benedict's judgment, grumbling is the most serious sin in the monastery. Twelve times he emphatically warns against *murmuratio*; he refers particularly to creating the occasion for grumbling, often by leaders. This does not mean that one may never speak up frankly and openly. Benedict is against the really poisonous grumbling and griping. Such grumbling works like a slow poison that penetrates the community. Grumblers look for one another and strengthen each another. Griping is like an undesirable "spiritual cell division" that sickens the community. However, there is an antidote: good words spoken well and cheerfully work like balm for the soul. For cheerfulness, courage is needed and it stimulates positive "spiritual cell division." Cheerfulness works infectiously and can help to tackle a difficult task or even a task that seems impossible. It would be easy to recall examples of cheerful people who even in a very difficult situation stimulate others to get busy in a good mood and with good courage—as grumblers succeed in sickening even a good situation or message and so sour it.

The listening spirituality of Benedict also teaches us in this respect how important it is to watch or mind one's words. We can speak bad words, *maledicere*, which sicken, insult, kill. We can speak good words, *benedicere*, which heal, make whole, bring life, bless. I shall return to this theme.

Thus, inside and outside the monastic world, Benedictine spirituality is not a beautiful but dead museum piece; it is a blessing. In a vital and attractive manner it invites one to live differently.

2

Reticence and Silence

In a culture of noise and chatter, a plea for silence does not seem to have much of a chance. Or is it precisely the attitude that is missed and for which we really are longing? The Benedictine Joan Chittister claims that silence is an element of monastic spirituality that has a contribution to make to our time. Everywhere we hear background rustling and not seldom, background noise: background music [*muzak*] in stores and nowadays even in buses, pulsing hard rock from cars (on the other hand, one seldom hears Vivaldi or Brahms from those sources of sound), jogging people with "headphones," loudly telephoning travelers in the train, noisy commercial messages that interrupt a subdued film, television hosts who noticeably turn up the volume with "nicer" topics (than did their predecessors twenty years ago), the television we do not turn off while we are busy with something else.

Monastic spirituality stands in sharp contrast to this. Monastic silence is not directed to forbid something negative, but to make something positive possible. According to Joan Chittister, that is expressed in small, everyday things:

Monastic spirituality calls us to live quietly. To walk quietly rather than to run. To close doors with knobs, rather than to push them closed. To speak directly to a person, rather than shouting to him in the hall. To turn down the volume rather than to raise it. To avoid noise pollution. To give the gift of silence to others as well.

This "gift" of silence may be contrasted with the dominant trait of our contemporary culture in many respects, which is instead characterized by greater volume and shouting. Impatient calling and noise pollution permeate society; the poison of noise instead of the gift of silence. What might a monastically inspired balm of quietness and silence mean for our culture?

Again, Joan Chittister:

Imagine what might happen in this country [the United States] if children did not live in homes where people shout at each other from early morning to late night. Imagine cities without bellowing and pounding music from screaming radios. Imagine our spirits if our final thought of the day were not inspired by a local television channel. Imagine if our lives, work and relationships, were not stupefied by noise and would not tremble from tension. Monastic silence is an antidote for the tumult which is created to distract us from the important things of life. Without silence monastic spirituality cannot become a yeast which makes our life rise.

Monastic silence is described with positive words like "gift" and "yeast," and not as punishment, a ban on speaking or penance. Instead of what outsiders think, this is not about "not being allowed to speak" but about "being allowed to be silent" and the respecting of the silence of others. A good illustration of this difference could be seen in one of the episodes of *The Monastery*, referred to above, the well-known series in which five men stayed for forty days in an abbey. A few participants concocted a naughty plan to break out of the monastic discipline. During the so-called night silence after Compline (the closing prayer celebrating the day) they left the area of the abbey for some drinks and smokes in a pub. They arrived home late and rang brother porter out of bed to be admitted again.

The following morning Abbot Christopher Jamison invited the "disturbers of the peace" for a conversation in his room. The producer of the series, as he told later in an interview, excitedly rubbed his hands because of what seemed like an impending conflict. He expected that the abbot would address these men in a firmly punitive voice. It turned out to be quite different. Abbot Christopher once more explained quietly and calmly the *sense* of certain aspects of monastic discipline. They were intended to offer the preconditions in which people and the community might experience a monastic culture and grow in it. The virtue of silence is not a prohibition against speaking; it rather promotes a climate of quietness and modesty. Precisely for this climate monks and guests have come to the monastery.

Silence does not mean that we close ourselves off in a sterile manner from any sound, but that we may open ourselves to what presents itself in our soul. The night silence that is maintained in the monastic world between Compline and the Lauds (morning service) offers a climate of rest that affects the entire house, in which people can read in a concentrated manner or have extra room for personal prayer and for a good night's rest. Those who disturb this climate cheat themselves and their fellow brothers.

In a study day about the film *De grote stilte* [*Into Great Silence*], in which almost without a text the life of monks from *La Grande Chartreuse* is registered, I heard interesting thoughts about the role of silence and refraining from speech.

The philosopher Charles Vergeer commented on their relation: they mutually differ, but they are also related. One can be silent or demand silence of someone else, but silence overcomes a person. Silence needs to fall, we cannot get hold of it; it is experienced and always contains a moment of surrender. The context of being silent can be helpful with that, but it surely does not guarantee the "falling" of silence. Silence in moments where speaking is suitable may generate a lot of noise, excitement, and aggression in people.

Of course, there are aids to create silence. Rituals may play a fruitful role in this. Quite surprisingly, silence can be stimulated by sound. With the Dutch national memory of the dead on May 4, on the Waalsdorpervlakte near The Hague, the ringing of the bell introduces a period of two minutes of silence. The connotation and the intensity of the silence is strengthened by this, followed by the closing trumpet. When there is silence for a few minutes in our abbey after the sung psalmody before the reading of Scripture, that silence is of a different nature than when I sit silently in the chapel for a few minutes—which I also do with pleasure. At the end of Compline the light in the chapel is turned off. It is almost dark when we sing a hymn to Mary. One of the brothers walks to the bell outside the chapel and makes it ring three times, separated by periods of silence.

At that point the night silence begins—the climate in the house has really changed from what it was earlier during the day in the monastery. Outside the monastery also, rituals may be devised that cultivate a caesura between the hours of the day.

In his meditation, Charles Vergeer has shown that fruitful silence must be measured. It is about a silence that does not oppress but that *may* create space. Something may appear in that space: epiphany, when what appears shines *through* us. A signal from another world? Or the same world appearing in a different light?

Peter Nissen, my colleague in church history, a Benedictine oblate with affinity for the spirituality of the Carthusians, also contributed to this study day about silence. The title of his contribution was expressive: "Living and Praying in the Eye of the Storm." It is calm in the "eye of the storm," but all around you see the wind blow. Male and female Carthusians seek silence, remote places where they cultivate lives of silence and prayer. But they know that it can storm violently on the outside, in "the world." In the spirituality of the Carthusians, silence is also an (important) precondition but not a goal. For in the eye of the storm something may appear, and that is the goal.

Moreover, the silence of the Carthusians is not complete. They speak together in a relaxed manner during weekly recreation, a conversation that can be pleasant and spiced with laughter.

Those who saw *Into Great Silence* probably also remember the most relaxed moment in the film, during the Sunday walk in the snow, with carefree silliness. Carthusians certainly also know about "the world," according to Peter Nissen. At a certain moment during their recreation, the brothers wished the Dutch prior a good journey to Seoul in connection with the recent construction of a second Carthusian monastery in South Korea. Earlier, a Carthusian monastery was established in South America in response to an express request of the bishops there. They realized all too well that the situation on that continent demanded active pastoral concern, but realized at the same time that an "eye of the storm" was needed within which silence could be cultivated.[6]

What is here on the micro-level is also in everyone's microcosmos. The storms in our lives and around us cannot be ignored—that would be a lack of realism—but our dealing with them gains in quality when we regularly "live and pray in the eye of the storm."

Benedict also underscores the importance of measured silence as a precondition for a good personal and social climate in a monastic community as a precondition for spiritual openness.

What do we read in the Rule?

We frequently meet in the Rule indications concerning the prudent dealing with the word and the cultivating of a climate of silence, attention, and concentration. Additionally, Benedict has dedicated a separate chapter (RB 6) to this. It has a place between the chapters on obedience and humility. It should be clear that these virtues are related. The three related monastic basic attitudes proceed in principle to the practical about the conduct of life in the community, which is regulated in the further text. All monastic life apparently needs to be seasoned by these three virtues. It is good to reflect that this is also valid for those who are chosen from the community to give leadership. The abbess and the abbot are subject to the Rule and are thus to cultivate their own obedience, silence, and humility.

The text of the chapter on silence is brief enough to quote in its entirety:

On Silence

1. Let us do what the prophet says: "I said: I will watch my ways that I might not sin with my tongue. I have placed a guard at my tongue; I have not spoken, but have been modest and have been silent even concerning good things."

2. Here the prophet points out that one must sometimes avoid good conversation for the sake of the great importance of silence, but is seldom given permission for conversation; one surely must avoid bad conversation because of the punishment that follows that sin.

3. Therefore, perfect students, on account of the great importance of silence, will seldom be given permission for conversation, even when it relates to good, holy, and fruitful conversation.

4. For it is written: "With much conversation, one cannot avoid sin."

5. And elsewhere: "The tongue has power over death and life."

6. Speaking and teaching is, however, the task of the master; students need to be silent and listen.

7. If one needs to ask something of the superior, one needs to ask with all humility and respectful submission.

8. Tasteless jokes, however, and all talk that only serves to generate laughter, we reject always and everywhere and we do not permit that a student open his mouth for such talk.

The usage of language (for example, the notions of "sin," "punishment," "humility," and "submission") and sometimes the content of some verses may perhaps repulse a contemporary reader. But after overcoming this small psychological barrier this chapter can—surely, as seen within the whole of the Rule—present us with a few matters worthy of reflection and particularly of practicing.

The Latin *taciturnitas* may be translated as reticence or keeping silent. The translator, Father Frans Vromen, claims that both meanings are possible in Late Latin. Reticence is more of an acquired attitude; keeping silent may be commanded or prescribed. Reticence as a conscious avoiding of speaking may be, in view of the context, also negative and damaging—in English it is sometimes associated with surly reticence. Benedict cannot have had such an attitude in mind.

Silentium is to be translated with "silence," as in the first place quietness by and among people. The request *silence, please*, would be suitable, for example, at the beginning of a concert or a lecture but would be rather ridiculous to request of a stormy sea or a flight of geese.

With the "prophet" in the first verse of this chapter, the psalmist is meant. Benedict cites here Psalm 39:2-3. The image of the guard at the mouth we also read in Psalm 141:3: "Set a guard over my mouth, O LORD; keep watch over the door of my lips." The psalmist (and Benedict) surely knew the experience that "we need to watch our words," and that, if we don't, we can create a lot of havoc, including things we ourselves value. Contemporary readers will easily recognize this.

A guard at my mouth: I have often intended it myself and have often noted the psalm verse in small handwriting on my notes before a meeting. I have shared in such meetings to serve "the agenda," rather than to "score" quickly on the point that is important to me and to build up my ego. Our speaking in consultation, according to Benedict, needs to be "humble." That is something other than servile or docile. Humility, as we will study in a subsequent chapter, deals with the "courage to serve."

The advice to speak reticently even about good things might possibly estrange us even more. Yet this advice also is related to humility and prudence.

The good often does not need explanation. After all, it is about the quality of the "good things," and not about our speaking about them. With speaking, one may pollute the good or even destroy it by talk. We can easily imagine situations when a beautiful accomplishment of a colleague (or of you yourself) quickly loses its admirable quality because it is exaggerated and related to pretenses.

And this is only one way in which our speaking can become sinful—by sullying what without these words would have been quite in order. My father would have sighed in his butcher shop with the botching up of prime usable meat: "Isn't that *zund* [sin]."

A second way our tongue can create harm is by the conscious infecting of social communication with "evil words." But as Benedict cites from the book of Proverbs, the tongue can bring both death and life. Words can harm, but they can also bless. We shall return to this theme in a closing chapter. In any case, Benedict's chapter on silence may impress on us that the quality of our speaking is determined by the quality of our silence.

Verses 6 and 7 of this chapter at first sight deal simply with the relations between master and teacher, and between superior and subordinate. Here the order clearly indicates everyone's place. But if we refer to the Rule as a whole, things appear more nuanced. The master and the superior also remain "in the teaching" of Christ, of the Scriptures, and also of the fellow brothers. Sometimes it is precisely the superior who needs to listen alertly, for example, particularly to the younger members of the community, or to the remarks of an unfamiliar monk from distant regions who is a guest. Again, humility must be primary: to serve well as master and superior you need to command a courageous attitude to give preference to advice and words from others above your own supposed insights and ever limited range of experience. At that point silent listening both by the master and the superior is fitting.

In the closing verse of his chapter on silence, Benedict dismisses *tasteless* jokes. I like to imagine that true wit can only occur with style, and that true wit in no way needs to be opposed to serious spiritual life. Talk that *only* aims at generating laughter and then often at the expense of the one talked about must be dismissed, however. Humor unifies and warms people. When tasteless jokes make someone ridiculous, the community is chilled and driven apart. There is an analogy here between concentrated silence, which can promote personal and social unity and devilish noise, which drives apart and disintegrates.

In her commentary on the Rule, on this chapter, Benedictine Michaela Puzicha refers to a relevant early Christian one-liner: *Diabolus sonum quaerit, Christus silentium*—"The devil looks for noise, Christ for silence."

The erudite author C. S. Lewis might have thought of this when he wrote his both witty and provocative *The Screwtape Letters* (also translated into Dutch). In this book, an older, experienced devil gives advice to a younger colleague, who, with insufficient subtlety, tries to seduce people. One of the advices of the experienced *Screwtape* is to stimulate a climate of noise and tumult, for noise is a good context and medium for the devilish work of seduction. Noise diffuses, with the result that the attention decreases. In this connection *Screwtape* also advises to avoid contexts of silence or soft, beautiful music, for they are counterproductive.

As always, this chapter of the Rule about silence must be seen in relation to the further text of the Rule. Then it becomes clear that speaking is definitely needed, meaningful, and wholesome. With work, conversation may be required not only, for example, for reasons of safety but also to learn from others. One speaks with guests, even if within set limits, as will be discussed below. In my own experience in the abbey, the conversation during daily dishwashing sessions is one of the most social moments of the day, even if it is less spectacular. New visitors find in these dishwashing sessions a context in which they are reassured in a natural manner, when they still need to get accustomed to the "strange" surroundings. The monks who are assigned to dishwashing (and others who are walking in and out) exchange experiences with the faithful visitors and hear what keeps them busy. Not surprisingly, at the end of the job they take their time with the washing-up of the towels.

In the brothers' counsel, speaking and listening are essential. Quite a few communities have conversations on a regular basis that do not deal with decision making about important matters, but they serve to promote mutual communication. The conversation is then between brothers and their fellow brothers who bear extra responsibility, such as the abbot, the prior, the cellarer, and the novice master. The cellarer, for example, must quietly listen even to unreasonable requests. When he needs to refuse a request, that is done in a reasonable manner, while he tries to add a "good word" as well.

Benedict also finds a conciliatory conversation between brothers important. Conciliation should preferably happen before nightfall.

In addition, the monastic tradition is acquainted with the constructive and friendly mutual conversation. My favorite example is beautifully expressed in *Over de spirituele vriendschap* [About Spiritual Friendship] by the twelfth-century Cistercian abbot Aelred of Rievaulx. This most profound tractate about friendship since Aristotle was written entirely in conversational form. Of course, Aelred has "composed" this, but one feels that real conversation was the foundation of this and that genuine experiences of friendship must have been its existential basis. The reader, the present reader at any rate, sometimes feels as if he could touch Aelred and his friend together in the monastic garden. We understand that Aelred must end the friendly conversation because the brother economist is coming, undoubtedly with "urgent business" for Abbot Aelred, who, after all, led a community of hundreds of brothers and who had to visit many foundations.

Do Benedict's lessons about silence (and suitable speaking) offer insights that might apply to non-monastic contexts? The most honest course for me to take is to limit myself to some personal experiences. Everyone's personal situation offers opportunities for finding a suitable balance between silence and speaking. I experience as salutary a silent beginning of the day, a silent half hour during the afternoon, and a silent close of the day (possibly in the form of quieting music). At my work I try to alternate periods of silent study, writing, and preparation for teaching (all of this with a telephone and answering machine, with the door of my room closed) with availability for (telephone) conversation and contact via electronic mail. Beside moments of formal consultation, informal contact may also be cultivated. The probably very "Dutch" custom of coffee drinking with colleagues sometimes offers more possibilities to signal matters and to set them in motion than the fixed "discussion on progress" in the minutes. Thus, an informal lunch with managing advisors and officers offers a good opportunity to fruitfully explore possibilities. But here the art of "the capacity for distinction" is fitting—what to speak about and what to avoid? In whatever form, silence and the quality of conversation are important preconditions for the quality of communal life.

Silence at meals in the monastery is not a disciplinary rule but a precondition for extra spiritual nurture. This may also be translated according to one's own situation. Sometimes I just read the newspaper with my silent breakfast, but on Sundays and holidays I find the weekend paper too "noisy" and I read a brief philosophical or spiritual text with it. I can imagine that people who live alone do well enjoying their meals in a climate of silence (or soft music) seated at a table rather than with the loud presence of the television.

The first experiences of guests in monastic silence are quite "mixed." Silence is not only experienced as positive. Abbot Christopher Jamison mentions in this connection the superficial calmness the monastic sphere elicits, which initially works as reassuring and beneficial. But when the silence lasts longer, the "demons" sometimes get free play—the trick is then "to stay in your cell," as was the advice in the past. The outer noise is replaced by inner unrest. This can only be "kept out," until it (sometimes) disappears.

Benedictine Johanna Domek writes about this:

Internal noise, internal conversation can exhaust us. Probably many people flee from this inner noise in the distraction of outside background noises and prefer to allow themselves to be overrun by this. But if you wish to grow spiritually, you need to remain in the room of your spiritual din and persevere and precisely there gradually come to rest, quietly and honestly remain in God's presence, till these voices dim little by little and your heart is gradually cleansed and silenced.

After that a deeper calmness can come about. But becoming silent cannot succeed by a quickly acquired technique. A "silent soul" is not easily acquired. So many things are at first sight attractive possibilities for escape that lead us from a silent and concentrated life—even in our monastic cell.

The Trappist Michael Casey sometimes connects the silence of monastic life with a form of psychotherapy known by the abbreviation REST (= Restrictive Environmental Stimulation): "A therapy in which one is consciously striving for a spiritual milieu of life with limited outside stimuli."

Also, monastic life is intentionally *unexciting* and aims for a climate of "creative monotony":

> The goal of a quiet life needs to be clear: it aims to promote a restful, calm spirit where spiritual priorities become more and more dominant. This withdrawal is not an invitation to isolation and navel-gazing. Rather, it wishes to grant the possibility to penetrate deeper into reality and to live from the heart.

It is therefore about a lifestyle with few stimuli, precisely in order to live a *more intense* spiritual life.

The longing for a quiet life with sensibly scheduled periods of silence and being alone, in which patience and calmness are cultivated, is found attractive by a remarkable and growing number of people. And then not like a little gimmick or a studied attitude, but from the heart, a heart that has tasted that a life in quietness, *to sit quietly with the Lord*, provides energy and vitality and space to breathe. The giving up of superficial excitement is then not a "penance" but a blessing. Abbot Christopher Jamison calls that *a lack of busyness*, a life without commotion. This is a life in which we are not hunted (not by ourselves, either), free from obsession, in which we live almost childlike in the "present."

In a culture of fragmentation, *multitasking*, and permanent diversion by many people, the longing grows for a quieter, more concentrated and sounder life.

An impressive testimony about this was written by Leo Fijen, who is busily occupied as television host and director of the RKK/KRO (Dutch Catholic television) program *Kruispunt* [Cross Point]. Through the years he made a widely watched and appreciated series about monastic life in the Netherlands and Europe.

There gradually arose thereby a deeply personal longing to live more slowly and differently. He spoke about this with the former abbot of the Trappist abbey of Koningshoeven, Korneel Vermeiren. Actually Leo hoped that the abbot would submit a "rule of life," but Leo rightly found that the "rule of life for Leo Fijen" needed to be discovered and be written by Leo Fijen himself. To discover that rule of life, the abbot sent Leo on a journey to Dutch seekers of God who offer leadership in Europe to monastic communities. After returning, he spoke again with Abbot Korneel. In their conversation they arrived at ten dimensions of a better regulated life for Leo Fijen—and, of course, for many others. This journey resulted again in an impressive series of programs and also in a beautiful personal book in which Leo Fijen described his journey of discovery of his own rule of life. The tenth aspect of his rule of life is simply called: "You need to become silent."

How does this busy "media man" do this himself? Again, very simply: with a quiet half hour in the morning. Rise a bit earlier, not tuning in to television, quietly empty the dishwasher, sitting still with a beautiful text. Not spectacular, and after that the hectic routine begins again. But according to his experience that quiet half hour accompanied the entire day and remained to nurture in the midst of all busyness.

It is attested spiritual advice both to schedule this silence and sometimes to increase it somewhat, to the extent it is personally possible. For example, a daily quiet half hour, a weekly quiet evening, a monthly quiet day, every quarter a quiet weekend at a place suitable for that, and annually a quiet week. Of course, the form and content of such a "program of silence" need to fit what is possible for someone and is socially suitable.

A friend, a busy communication advisor, has indeed such a monthly quiet day, but not directly in a monastic context, so I noted once at the Nijmegen station where I met him in a walking outfit. "Vacation?" was my logical question. "No, this is my monthly walking day. I travel by train to a beautiful area for walking, this time not where I go for my vacation and without my partner and walk an entire day in silence. This keeps me going."

Finally, it is good to emphasize that this "keeping one going" is not only related to personal psychic health. The fruits of silence, of economical and sensible use of words, are both personal and social, and hopefully become visible in daily life together. For example, with greater patience in listening comes a greater responsibility for the words of others and a realistic awareness that one does not always have to have the last word. One's silence and speaking *serve* a purpose. The Benedictines would say: they are imbedded in "humility," in the courage to serve.

3

Humility: The Courage to Serve

In the Rule of Benedict, chapters 5, 6, and 7 are dedicated to three basic monastic attitudes, in which the practical matters that follow—the Holy Office of choir prayers, organization of life, correction of non-monastic behavior, tasks and functions—need to be done and experienced. This is about obedience, heightened in this chapter in the relationship with the superior, silence, and humility. To Benedict, these attitudes are close together. The first verse of chapter 5 reads: "The first step of humility is obedience without delay." When silence must be broken, so he claims in chapter 6, humility is again fitting: "If one needs to ask the superior something, the asking is to be done with all humility and subjection." In the chapter on humility, obedience (in the second and third "step") and silence (in the ninth and eleventh "step") are mentioned again.

Benedict must have seen humility as just as important, as well as a difficult virtue to own: he spends the longest chapter of his Rule on it, a chapter of no less than seventy verses (for obedience and silence he needs respectively nineteen and eight verses). The word *humilitas* occurs seventy-one times in the Rule; it is apparently a crucial concept.

With a first reading, the contemporary reader of this chapter encounters several things that seem strange, unhealthy, even shocking: the fear of God who ever watches us from heaven (which is rather less frightening, however, if it is seen as a loving, motherly view); not being allowed to do your own will; not following your own longings; enduring hard, unpleasant, and even unjust things; confessing your bad thoughts to the superior; viewing yourself as an incompetent and unworthy worker; seeing yourself as the least important of all; speaking softly without laughing; a humble posture with a downcast view. What do we do with this in a culture that rightly sees free choice, independence, self-development, profiling, and assertiveness as important characteristics? Or is humility just something that in a culture of macho behavior, ambition, competition, rivalry, livening up, "spin," and "showing off" might be something worthwhile? The contrast with the place Benedict grants to humility is, in any event, very great. That must certainly have been the case in his late ancient context. He built communities where rivalry and competition were lacking. Monks, he claims, may only compete together in one area: in showing respect for one another. That appears to be a valuable attitude even outside monasteries.

Moreover, monks owe not only obedience and respect to their superiors but also to one another. Superiors and other leaders need to listen with an affectionate heart to fellow brothers and sisters, not in the least also to the younger ones, to visitors from a distance, and to the weak. This must have been a strictly new communal order in Benedict's times, a community in which no single member is central. The life of the community circles around a center consciously kept "empty" and "nonproductive" (the original meaning of the word *templum*), an emptiness filled by the daily hymn to the glory of God.[7] It is quite remarkable that a communal life permeated by humility may be attractive in an aggressive world, in Benedict's time and ours.

When investigating the meaning of a concept, it is often a good beginning to check to see how it is used in our language. At the word "humility," Van Dale, the Dutch lexicographer, comments (translated): "subjection," "mood of humble submission," "opposite of pride." Synonyms of "humble" are indicated as: "unpretentious," "of low descent," "modest," "meek," "humble." With "humility" the religious dimension is also mentioned: "knowing oneself dependent on God." In the commentary on the Rule by Michaela Puchiza the etymological root is also named—the Old High German *diomuoti*: "the courage to serve." In advance of the subsequent discussion it may be mentioned that Benedict is particularly concerned with these last two dimensions. Both dimensions we might call "ex-centric": the one that the monk targets and the one that is central for him—God, who, is "highly" esteemed; however, he shows himself particularly in the fellow brother, the guest, the task that lies before you, the text to which you have listened with a receptive heart. The monk knows himself to be "in service." The center of his inclination lies outside his "ego." This is, of course, recognized by anyone who has experience with interpersonal affection. But apart from the two named dimensions that many of our contemporaries also judge positively, the semantic field of "humility" and the content of the seventh chapter of the Rule still contains much of what goes against the grain with us in our first and even frequent rereading. This is not only the experience of "outsiders" who have learned to appreciate much in the remainder of the Rule, but also of people from the monastic world who have listened to this chapter three times a year.

Vincent Hunink, who gave us the most recent Dutch translation of the Rule, told at a meeting of the Merton friends about the inward resistance he felt when he was translating this chapter.[8] Both in the word *humilitas* and in the content in which Benedict gives humility such a central place, he found himself being confronted. The word said nothing to him, "in any case nothing positive. As far it did say something to him, it was negative: humility as a bit awkwardly, unworldly, uncomfortably self-effacing." Additionally, he noted an ironic meaning, for example, when you call your grand villa "your humble mini-cot." Neither that negative connotation, nor the ironic undertone he felt to be fitting in his translation project deterred him, for he wished to let the Rule of Benedict speak to contemporary readers. If he wished to achieve that, such a key concept needed to be insightful, understandable, and recognizable. Thus, in the first versions of his translation he used a term with a more positive emotional value, "simplicity." But that quickly became troublesome; to humble oneself is truly something else than to simplify. Moreover, the biblical references Benedict used produced problems as well. Vincent Hunink also tried such concepts as "singularity," "simplicity," and "modesty," but these also began to pinch. Moreover, his (sometimes monastic) readers blew the whistle on him. That set a process in motion that is remarkably illustrative of what *humilitas* may contain. Originally, he received the difficult advice to stay away altogether from the term "humility." However, that is the way it reads, that is the meaning, whether you find it nice or not, and that is how it needs to be translated. "That was hard advice. But I have accepted the lesson of my readers, first reluctantly and resentfully, later somewhat happily and finally even without complaining." Gradually, he experienced this process as personally putting into practice precisely that *humilitas* and as almost literally going down on one's knees before that old stubborn word in an old stubborn text, a word that he at first wanted to remove because of personal sensitivities. Translating is also "ex-centric," the text and its context are central, not the translator.

That is what Vincent Hunink also noted regarding the content of the seventh chapter. Not only the word *humilitas*, but the entire chapter was offensive to him, "something to abhor," and "a bitter pill for a modern person." No wonder he struggled for a long time with this chapter. However, just like with the word *humilitas*, part of his resistance ebbed away. He realized that he had to struggle with it if he was to take his translation project seriously. What helped him was partially the text itself:

> It begins with all kinds of terrible texts, but it becomes even worse . . . . Every time you think: now we hit bottom, it cannot get worse! And then it takes another step

down, still deeper into humiliation. At a certain moment
I thought: well, it has to go this way, I'll have to go down
into the depths with the text . . . and drink the bitter
chalice to the end. Fortunately, at the end there are a few
texts that suddenly look quite nice, which are not quite
so hard. At the eleventh and the twelfth step, it seems as
if man is suddenly liberated, as if the lowest humiliation
brings liberation with it. I have experienced this in going
along with the text. This ancient text is greater and older
than I, more worthy of respect than I am, and even if I do
not understand it, I'll have to go along with it.

That appeared to be a liberation for the translator. He compares
it to radical musical experiences: "[A] musical wealth which is
so great that it makes me into a very small man. This transcends
your personal feeling. You go down on your knees and yet remain
standing as a person. It does not harm your dignity, you remain
totally intact."

In monastic circles also, the seventh chapter of the Rule gen-
erates understandable irritation among contemporary readers.
Once in a course I gave to a community of nuns, I brought up
this chapter. Particularly among the older sisters I noted quite a
bit of resistance, naturally camouflaged quite courteously in the
good Benedictine tradition. For, of course, the virtue (a virtue is
always an acquired attitude of *excellence*, according to Aristotle)
of humility is often distorted and perverted in a sour mental-
ity in which people are belittled and kept small. However, the
chapter on humility was not at all meant to do someone in and
keep them small, but to teach small and limited little people
(who we all are) to grow to their true (and not their imagined)
grandeur. The seventh chapter of the Rule is a "growth chapter."
In the comments of Vincent Hunink we could already hear this
dynamic. Toward the end of the text a liberating tone is sounded,
and after the twelfth step of humility stands an almost laughing
Christ awaiting the monastic man who has grown according to
his true (not his imagined) length and figure [*gestalte*]. This last
point is the key to reading this text. I have read this chapter from

the end to the beginning with the community of nuns, starting at the joyful end and reading back to the point of departure. Benedict's starting point is an apparent cold but realistic shower in which he first makes us understand "in a good and proper manner" who we are: little people before each other and before the face of God, little people with limitations and boundaries, but with an unsuspected and lifelong potential for growth to be developed. Just as in the whole of the Rule, Benedict wishes to call us to become what we truly can be.

The chapter about humility must be seen as an exercise in realism. Humility is about a realistic view of the place (or rather, the little place) that you occupy in reality. *Humilitas* is openness and respect for reality as well as for ourselves. We are not the "owner" of it. In the monastic tradition, *humilitas*, *realitas*, and *veritas* are therefore connected concepts. Truth and reality are seen in contrast with appearance and illusion. Benedict is against appearance and illusion and for reality and a realistic picture of ourselves.

This stands in a tense relation to our need for applause, the spotlight, and success, and to our aversion to critique and correction.

Growth in humility is growth in integrity and truthfulness, and this process is accompanied by irritation and pain. Benedict also emphasizes that we need help with this birth process. Others may act as "midwife," they can assist with the liberating "exodus" out of our illusions to our realistic but true "grandeur." The spirituality of Benedict, says Anselm Grün, is not a pessimistic spirituality. The inner way the monk must walk is a spiritual process of ripening. No apathy belongs with this ripening process, no oppressions, passive acceptance, and "organized" humiliation. It is a positively oriented way in which he must go.

Twelve Signposts on the Way of Humility

The chapter about humility places a number of signposts on this route. These signposts wish to ascend to God, but they are at the same time a descent into one's own reality. For Grün, *humilitas* also connects with the acceptance of one's own humanity.

Which signposts does Benedict place on this road that needs to be walked again and again? He distinguishes twelve steps of humility that are succinctly summarized here in notations consciously expressed in a bit more up-to-date (and perhaps in a more acceptable) manner, yet do justice to the spirit in which Benedict writes:

1. Fearing God;

2. Not loving your own will;

3. Obeying your superiors from the love of God;

4. Tolerating hard and even unrighteous treatment with courage and patience;

5. Realizing and recognizing your own mistakes;

6. To be able to have peace with barren, even poor circumstances, without thinking that you deserve better;

7. Being grateful to God that our self-satisfaction and conceit have been punctured;

8. Following the example of experienced fellow brothers rather than our own conceit;

9. Choosing and weighing our words carefully;

10. Not being superficial and jesting unfittingly;

11. Being mild mannered, serious, modest, and reasonable in our use of language and

12. In all our behavior.[9]

Even formulated thus, these aspects of humility will call forth resistance from many. Yet everyone will sense that cultivating steps eight up to and including twelve might cheer up our life together even outside the monastic context and that steps five through seven, though they are admittedly difficult processes, might do our psychic health some good.

Benedict prefaced these twelve steps by a few introductory and relevant remarks, chiefly consisting of biblical quotes. He reminds us of the remarkable paradox that it is precisely the one who exalts himself who will be humbled, and the reverse. He relates this to the metaphor of Jacob's ladder (Gen 28:10-17). Just like the angels who appeared in Jacob's dream, we can ascend to the heavenly spheres in this earthly life, but then we descend by our pride as we ascend by our humility. Pride sounds at once heavy and sinful. Some among us by nature enjoy taking a high flight, but then we notice in a painful manner that this high flight will be possible only if we first strike deep roots and are achieving sufficient growth whereby a realistic awareness of our shadowy sides belongs to our nature.

An abbot once said about a fellow brother, who after a restless, searching life inside, outside, and again inside the monastery, had grown to be a fruitful prior who stimulated others: "Brother Aad was a real high flyer. Thus he has had to pass through deep valleys." This is a double dynamic. It is not about valleys only; it is about going down in order to *rise*. This is how Joan Chittister put it in her commentary on the Rule: "Humility consists in knowing who we are and knowing for which harvest our life is destined. The irony of humility is that when we have gained it we also know our grandeur and know that we are destined for God."

Benedict further compares the rungs of the ladder with body and soul: humility, if it should not wish to climb in a crooked manner and fall, must ascend evenly in our inward and outward behavior.

The Twelve Steps Examined Closer

The First Step: The Fear of God

Monks and nuns are, as are all Christians, seekers of God and followers of Christ, whether they walk this path of life within a very specific structure or not. The first step underscores that monastic life is hetero-centric: the Other is central, and the Other often has the face of others, that of your fellow sisters, the superior, the guests. You need to regard them "highly." In their turn and in their own view, they themselves are not central, for the fellow sisters and the superior are also subject to the Rule and therefore as subject to this first step, which calls them to stand and to go hetero-centrically in life and in the community instead of egocentrically, and esteem others "highly." This paradoxically appearing mutual asymmetry must definitely have had the concurrence of the philosopher Emmanuel Lévinas. A friendly colleague (Jean Greisch) asked him during a journey on the train whether the famous saying by Martin Heidegger also pertained to him: "Thinking is the limiting to a single thought, which once will remain standing as a star in the sky of this world." Emmanuel Lévinas formulated his own one star in a little sentence of three words: "*Autrui me regarde*"—which in French has a double meaning: "the other watches me," but also (for Lévinas at least as important): "the other concerns me." Humility is concerned with a deep respect for mystery and the high value of the other.

This is precisely what Benedict expresses when he says in the first step: "The first step of humility consists in this, that one always keeps the fear of God in view and thus is always on guard against forgetfulness." The "fear of God" is a biblical expression for a respectful (and loving) relationship of dependence between me and the other/Other and not for a traumatizing relation of subjection. It should immediately be affirmed, however, that this perverting of the respectful and loving relationship of dependence has caused many traumas in monastic life (and outside it). The *timor Dei* is not depressing but liberating. Cassiodorus, the early church father, remarks in this connection: "Fear of people makes you a slave, the fear of God sets you free." Further in the text of this first step Benedict encourages the monk to think that he "needs to be convinced that God watches him always from heaven . . . ." Older readers will recall this passage about the picture of God's all-seeing eye, mounted in a triangle, sometimes displayed in strategic places in their school building to prevent possible naughty behavior. God's view is thus seen as the view of a frightening Superspy, a Big Father who has placed us under the permanent spiritual view of a camera.

This is also a perversion, for God sees us with a gentle view, the joyful and loving view of the father who has left the house to festively welcome his returning son who was not virtuous, and who during the festival goes outside again to meet the mocking elder son (who was always virtuous, but not at this time) with good words. Both sons learn what humility means: to gain a different view on reality.

Also for those who do not see themselves as seekers of God and followers of Christ, the named relationship of dependence is, in a certain sense, well known. We are not independent; we do not keep ourselves standing and going. We are fed by external sources. Quite often these sources are people with whom we are connected in affection, whom we esteem "highly." Humility at its best, claims the Dominican Timothy Radcliffe in an address to a Congress of Benedictine Abbots, is the gradually penetrating realization "that you not only are not the center of the world but that you are not even yourself the center of yourself."

Benedict is not concerned with self-realization but with self-transcendence. For, oddly enough, Trappist Michael Casey claims, care for others does not lead to the diminishing of your soul; it rather allows it to come to fruitful growth. We ourselves grow and prosper best when we serve the other and the other thing, and apply ourselves to that.

The Second Step: A New Orientation of Our Will

This is not about a striving for lack of will, but a turn of the will to join itself in a connection we deem to be higher. It is a task of the impulsive self-seeking will and the exercise of the (sometimes heavy) listening to the other, so that they knowingly seek the other.

Blind, thoughtless obedience is really not a free choice. The obedience that Benedict urges on us, we choose with full understanding, so says Abbot Christopher Jamison. But it is a difficult choice that needs to be made again and again.

The Third Step:
Obeying One's Superior—From the Love of God

Obedience, we read in this step, has its place within a context of love. Monastic obedience without this supporting element becomes, says Abbot Guillaume Jedrzejczak of Katsberg, an idiotic masquerade. In a community, people are thus quickly tempted to withdraw by themselves, to build up their own well-protected little world, there "to do their own thing." When this happens, the vitality of the community chills and shrivels. I have the impression that in many organizations that are not monastic communities, comparable processes occur. To the virtue of humility belongs the orientation of one's own will to what is valuable and to what is presented and handed to us from elsewhere. I must then learn to admit that I do not have the final answer, the best insight, for that would suggest I have finished growing. With the longing for growth belongs the readiness to listen—and that pertains, as was emphasized previously, to the superior.

Abbot Christopher cites in his book *Finding Sanctuary* a grandly organized American investigation of enterprises that in their history experienced a remarkable defining moment in which they changed from *good* to *great*. It was noted that the appointment of a certain type of "leader" coincided exactly with such a defining moment. It was always about administrative chairpersons who combined a profound personal humility with an intense professional vision and will. Benedict would have read this with approval.

The Fourth Step:
To Bear the Difficult Courageously and Patiently

The fourth step is that of *patientia, passio*, patience, bearing it.

This is about the patient and even-tempered acceptance of difficult and unpleasant things that will not be lacking: unfavorable circumstances, hurtful people. In a ripening process, the bitter parts will not be lacking. Such bitterness frequently asserts itself in the interpersonal sphere, in the relationship with fellow brothers and with those who provide leadership. This may be why some monastic humor has this experience of bitterness as its background.

"Question: What is the most difficult thing in the monastic life? Answer: Other monks." I once heard one of my fellow brothers say this.

"Question: Why does Benedict say that the abbot in the monastery is the substitute of Christ? Answer: Because he is the only whom we crucify." I read this is in an otherwise very sympathetic book of the Benedictine Andrew Nugent.

This rather dark humor fits well in the context of this fourth step. For Benedict expressly named two possible causes of bitter experiences inside the monastery: the superior who is appointed over us and who does "sometimes lay difficult, unpleasant things upon us," and some fellow brothers from whom "we have to endure all sorts of injustice." Benedict was a realist or certainly had become one and therefore knew that in everyday reality these situations will occur and need to be avoided. It is no different outside monasteries.

His advice is clear: exercise steadfastness, do not run away (also internally), stick with it, in short, practice *stabilitas*, not embittered, but literally "embracing" *patientia*. Three attitudes may help us: keeping silent, remaining patient, and creating space. In our culture, we probably cannot expect applause for this. We desire quick solutions, remedies for all problems, technically, as it were, brushing our stress away, removing obstacles. If that does not succeed, then we will become quickly irritated. Bearing patiently, allowing processes enough time, recognizing obstacles, persevering—that is Benedict's motto. Above all, it must not be teeth-gnashing perseverance; that would add another obstacle.

Benedict avers in this step also that you cannot solve anything on your own strength, but particularly because of the affection you meet unexpectedly—for which you need to be open—and by the affection toward others you try to keep alive in spite of bitter experiences. Just as the abbot must hate sin but must love the sinner, as is taught elsewhere in the Rule, this is true for the entire interpersonal communication in the community.

The Fifth Step:
Recognize Your Mistakes and Limitations

The fifth step teaches me that I must acknowledge that I cannot manage on my own. If I wish to grow, I need to be prepared to be honestly and openly in contact with others and thereby to acknowledge my weaknesses and accept their help and orientation. When your soul is growing it is important that you open your heart to your abbot or to an experienced and tested fellow brother. They can give you insight into your own reality and give you a word for your further travels. With the fifth step of humility you accept some "advice," again an attitude that contrasts with the spirit of our time. Benedict speaks here not only about the abbot as person to whom you need to tell your bad thoughts and hidden mistakes. In other chapters it is explained that trusty fellow brothers can also be good conversation partners in such things. Abbot Guillaume of Katsberg gives a possible motive in his commentary on the Rule for the fact that Benedict in this fifth step only mentions the abbot: for the one who had "tempted" the monk to think bad thoughts might, in many cases, have been the abbot himself.

And indeed, how much grumbling and how many feelings of misunderstanding and feelings of revenge are often generated in us by the words (or the silence) of our leaders? Benedict's advice: just say it, do not let it proliferate, do not bring it up in the community for dissemination. However, this is not about a confessional conversation—canon law forbids that the superior is the confessional priest to the brothers. This is rather about an honest conversation with another about the things that obstruct and cause pain.

This is easier said than done. How is this done, for example, if you do not have a good abbot? It happens. In that case, such a conversation does not work well and may cause more problems. This question was submitted once to Anselm Grün when he was in conversation with a group of leaders. He proposed a number of steps. When, for example, in a consultation with your "abbot" an unpleasant situation arises and words are said that hurt you, then first create some distance. Sit back and keep quiet. Look at this event like a play in which you now have a role you do not find very pleasing. Above all, do not begin a power struggle with your abbot, for you will lose that struggle. After the meeting, when you are back in the area where you give leadership, try to find a few partners for the plans you envision, which were turned down. Try to look together for the possibilities, within your own competences—not to develop anything against the abbot but to develop or create something you and your colleagues see as a *good* development. When the first good results appear in your departmental project, at a fitting moment (and in a good manner), tell the abbot about it. There is a good chance (not guaranteed, of course) that he will appreciate what you have developed.

Prioress Johanna Domek points out in her presentation that the goal of the spiritual road of Benedict is our becoming human, but "without putting your personal precipices in brackets . . ." Two coordinates are indicated here between which this can take place—by which heaven and earth are not separated: transparence and trust, in other words, confession and compassion.

The Sixth Step: Not Being Overly Demanding

The sixth step summons us, without any pretense, to dare to make our way toward freedom. This includes that you do not remain stuck and that you accept mobility on your life's path. This also includes being *content* with the least—thus, adopting a positive attitude toward the smallest, not ironically learning to live with it. Benedict pleads for a life free from ambition and fastidiousness, where we dare to stand poor before God and thus find freedom. In this connection he mentions the example of the Pharisee and the tax collector who stand before God in the temple, but with a totally different attitude—and a very different meeting with God. The Pharisee, who demands much from others and from himself (and is proud of that), sees himself as somebody important and of greater value than the tax collector in the back, who does not even look up, but is persuaded of what is lacking in his life and asks for mercy, which is forthcoming.

The Seventh Step:
Being Glad That Our Inflated Ego Has Been Punctured

This was the worst of the steps for Vincent Hunink. When he shared his own translation of these verses with the gathering of the friends of Merton mentioned above, he felt resentment arising again, and he told us:

> But that seventh chapter was indeed something horrible! I have now translated it as follows: "The seventh step of humility asks that you label yourself as worse and more worthless than all others and to really feel that deep inside. Humble yourself and say with the prophet: 'But I am a worm and not human; scorned by others, and despised by the people' (Ps 22:7); and also: 'It is good for me that I was humbled, so that I might learn your statutes' (Ps 119:71)." That is a bitter pill for a modern person—this is how I consider myself in any case. To be worse [to *label* yourself as worse in any case, WD], than all others, the least of all and feeling that inside—my entire being resists that. And when I say these words, it keeps doing that. This resentment has not left me entirely.

This reaction is quite understandable. Certainly when you read these words unprepared and unrelated to the rest of the Rule, they hardly communicate in a liberating way, not as a part of the way intended to lead to a blessed life and good days. Yet they are a part of it. Thus, there is nothing else to do than to read through what is at first sight unpleasant and shocking language and to try to give this seventh step a place in the whole of the chapter and in the whole of Benedict's project.

From the first step we have been shown our limits ever more deeply. We are now to realize truly that we represent little, but are only a human, and that we need to surrender all appearances from deep inside. The Trappist Michael Casey claims that humility as self-transcendence makes us into the antihero in the story of our life; often we simply do not know whether we are incompetent or if we just muddle along. To acknowledge this and to grow from our stubborn fiddling about demands a helpful effort and a powerful motivation. Humility does not demand perfection but honesty and patient helpfulness.

The context makes clear that this step aims at resisting competition on the basis of external status and position. That includes not measuring ourselves alongside others and overestimating ourselves. The counsel to esteem everyone higher than ourselves must be conceived in a healthy and positive manner. This is not about a masochistic cultivation of personal inferiority—that would be another perversion.

As an experienced and trusted abbot, Benedict must have known well that in a monastic community there occurs mutual comparison, jealousy, and camouflaged self-congratulation, in comparison with the newcomers. That is what this step opposes. Outside monastic walls there are, of course, well-known phenomena, such as pretentious behavior and being thick skinned.

Benedict peppers us with his pithy (biblical) words about our own fragility and limited capacities. That might also teach us respect for the fragility and limitations of our fellow brothers.

The Eighth Step:
Joining Yourself Willingly but Not Uncritically

This eighth step urges us to remain in contact with the common things and particularly with what tested and mature tradition hands us. That is good soil in which to grow. This is another attitude that contrasts with our culture, where we all are too quickly inclined to say or to think, "I can figure that out myself." Benedict advises the monk to concentrate first on the rules, traditions, and style of the house—which are not static data but need to be open to adaptations and changes. No originality is expected from the monk, but rather critical continuity, writes Michaela Puzicha in her commentary on this step.

Anselm Grün in this connection points to the experience of Henri Nouwen when he resided for half a year in the Trappist abbey of Genesee. The daily minimally exciting course of events makes him conscious of his need to always want to be special, the star. As a successful author and speaker he was able to satisfy that need very well. But in such an abbey there is no place for star-like airs, and he was therefore almost painfully confronted about his blustering inclination to be "someone special." Abbot John Eudes Bamberger helped him to discover this. This process is not directed to self-denial but toward self-discovery. Then one may discover that the treasure lies just in the soil of the everyday life, as Prioress Johanna Domek remarks apropos this step.

On the Ninth, Tenth, and Eleventh Steps: Carefully Minding One's Words and Not Making Anything and Anyone Ridiculous

The importance of silence and reticence was already discussed in an earlier chapter. Benedict's fundamental thought is just as simple as it is timeless: when I talk too much, I hear nothing. This is also true of the abbot; he should not want to be the Pavarotti of the community, always present and always talking. Benedict underscores here and also elsewhere how important it is to develop a feeling for the right moment of speaking, for the right moment for silence, and for the right "tonality" of your word (and undoubtedly also your silence).

Again, the contrast with our own culture (and probably also that of late ancient Rome, where Benedict studied for a time) is great. For example, how do we behave ourselves in situations of consultation? We feel good only after we have stated our piece. A meeting where we have not said anything, we regard as a failure. At the next meeting we look at the written minutes to see whether our words have been noted and transcribed correctly— what the others said, we read quickly, unless, of course, it refers to one of our concerns.

And who does not regularly in family conversation or among acquaintances experience the enslaving fascination of someone's own story that everyone needs to hear, sometimes three times in the same evening. One of my own sins is that I easily laugh and am good natured, ignoring something I would rather not hear and thus taking insufficiently seriously a problem my fellow workers bring to my attention. I should have been silent here and have minded my words instead of quickly conjuring up a whole series of power points. Was Benedict against good sense, joy of life, humor, radiant laughter, or even a quiet smile? One would almost think so, in view of his remarks in these steps (and also elsewhere): no enjoyable chatter, "not being inclined to laugh quickly," "speaking softly without laughter."

In the Psalter that every monastic community completes singing many times, there is a lot of jubilation, praise, and laughter (besides expressions of all other human emotions). Thus, Benedict could hardly have objected to that. His reservation pertains to laughter that hurts and always puts down a person (who may be absent) negatively and ridiculously. Benedict advises us to speak softly and sparsely, where dignity is never lacking—not even when the monks during recreation make playful foolishness in the snow around *La Grande Chartreuse*.

Over against that, he proposes a tempered reaction, without boisterousness, without pushing oneself ahead. The nuances he proposes in these steps and certainly the context of the whole of his Rule make it clear, however, that he definitely cannot have been a proponent of a "sour" and joyless monastic life. The whole is rather breathing a spirit of joyful dedication, in which humor does not need to be lacking.

He surely must have known that the words *humilitas*, *humus*, and *humor* belong to the same word family. Humility implies that you just keep standing with your feet in the *humus*, the earthly, and that you do not sing yourself loose from reality, as it were. When you should think that you might be able to float above the *humus* (and so in one way or another fall back), both the recognition of your own limits and their correction is more apt to happen in a climate of brotherly and sisterly humor than with military, disciplinary measures.

Some time ago I witnessed an interesting monastic example of that. I had literally experienced a fall on the beautiful marble steps that lead to the auditorium of our university medical center. I was about to give an introductory lecture on culture to about three hundred third-year medical students. I had done that in former years, and it had always been a great success with exultant student evaluations. I walked down the steps, thinking about a few new "brilliant" ideas on the theme of culture that would surprise the students. Meanwhile, I carried one bag in each hand, one with books and another quite heavy bag with "products of culture": a Bach score, a beautiful bronze statue of two monks sharing the peace, a screwdriver, a box with fresh "organic" eggs, which of course are provided with registration stamps by our culture and not by the chicken. Instead of carefully paying attention to the steps and to my balance, I hovered in higher, "brilliant" regions. *So* I fell with a bang (fortunately without serious hurt). The students were shocked and I had to give my lecture sitting at a table and shaking, instead of walking around the room, while acting to charm the class. And the eggs could, of course, not be shown anymore. A few days later I was at the abbey. Because of my injuries I walked with a cane. When leaving the chapel I was the last one out, behind the two eldest brothers, who also used canes. When they hung up their choir mantels, the one said: "Wil, welcome to the cane parade. What happened?" Then I told them about my fall and how it happened. The other one asked casually, "Surely you must have had proud thoughts?"—of course, because of the proverb: "Pride goes before the fall." But he hit the nail on the head. Fortunately, the almost ninety-year-old monk asked another sympathetic and interested question: "What did you really tell those boys and girls about culture?" But he had given me something to think about.

The Twelfth Step:
An Attitude of Humility Even to Its Smallest Details

The twelfth step points out that humility needs to be an attitude of both body and soul, and indeed with *everything* and *always*. Humility that is visible only in externals is not genuinely internalized. But if humility is to be genuine and fruitful in everyday life, it needs to be not only internal but also visible and audible in one's external behavior.

At the end of humility's ladder I always find myself in my everyday behavior, but raised up and liberated. There is no reward for my accomplishment, but a longing for grace that is silenced.

The lyrical coda of this chapter clarifies that the "top" of humility is not equivalent to being deeply depressed but reaches a level that is a joy to inhabit. For the language is now fully in a major key: without anxiety we go on our way to the love of God (*ad caritatem Dei*), from love to Christ (*amore Christi*), from joy in virtue (*bona et dilectatione virtutum*).

The steps of humility offer no blueprint for progress in the human drive to perfection; but they are pointers for the hearty opening of the ego to grow in freedom and love. It may happen in that process of growth that we, after a drudging, fearful, and sometimes bitter start, are led to a "delightful garden." Of course, this is a lifelong process we never complete. It is a process of transformation and growth in which these "steps" of humility really grow in a person's life, with a smiling Christ at the end, who, in John's gospel, is indicated as "the way, the truth, and the life." The road of humility is not a disparaging road but a road to truthfulness and a blessed life. It is a road that leads from the desert of the ego to the garden of a blessed life in which we together enjoy a new quality of life.

The intended liberating road of humility often leads to a new prison (that of the collective and a straitjacket of enslaving rules). Then, the difficult and heavy things that are unavoidable on that road became an independent goal, while real growth is hampered or even blocked—which is a real shame. The coda of the chapter about humility shows clearly what (or rather, who) must prevail. Moreover, the rest of the Rule shows that humility is an important, perhaps even the most important, basic attitude but certainly not the only one. Particularly, the pair of chapters Benedict added later breathes a spirit of warm brotherliness, mutual respect, affection between abbots and monks, a wise power of discernment about what the abbot asks of the brothers. One gets the impression that he, in a mild way, wishes to avoid that the discipline actually needed is sometimes derailed, so that the monastery becomes an emotional freezer and an enslaving prison instead of a warm breeding ground where people may become free.

Joan Chittister calls the virtue of humility, the courage to serve, a virtue that has become lost in our era, which cries to heaven to be rediscovered. The development of the nations, the preservation of the milieu of our life, and the perspective of the human community might well depend on it.

4

Blessed Work: A Benedictine View of Our Daily Work

When I once visited the Benedictine abbey where I am an oblate, the eldest brother (about eighty-five years old) took up table service that week. After the prayer by the prior and a brief Scripture reading by the person who was "reader of the week," the brother served the soup, fetched the ingredients of the second course from the kitchen on his little wagon, put them on the table, gathered the soup bowls and brought them to the kitchen to be washed, started to wash the dishes, returned later to collect the bowls of the main course and the dessert, and also brought them back. While monks and guests did the rest of the dishes after the meal, the aged table servant and the young weekly reader took their place in a brotherly manner beside one another to eat the meal that had been kept warm.

The table server did this work attentively the rest of the week without any signs of resentment or indignation about the fact that he, as old as he was, had to serve all kinds of young folk among the fellow brothers and the guests. The brother who had table service this week was also the one who had to ring the bell to wake the monks at quarter to six in the morning, before the first service in the chapel. Moreover, the first days of that week he took the place of the celebrant at the Eucharist, who, because of family reasons, had to be away from the monastery for a few days. Of course, he sang along in the service of readings, Lauds, afternoon service, Vespers, and Compline. The rest of the day he spent in meditation, study, personal prayer—and of course, recreation. He thus carried out a full program that did not burden him and that gave monks, and guests also, even to a very advanced age, breath and strength.

Some of his fellow brothers whom I have known died, as it were, "with their boots on"; the custodian and trusted advisor of people who asked for personal direction (he often stroke a little light for "dark" souls), the porter, the electrician, and technical jack-of-all-trades. A few others whom I have known and who now rest in the little monastery cemetery still carried out their responsibilities when they were more than eighty years old, before they had to lay them down because of sickness: the abbot, the sculptor who was also a chronicler. The man who was prior until 2005, who therefore provided daily leadership, was two years younger than the table servant of that week and also a well-read philosopher, a highly esteemed speaker about Ruysbroeck, and a teacher of meditation.

As to the permanent place of *work* in monastic life, people never go on pension, and "disabilities" do not occur. This is eloquently expressed in a story I read by an American monk. A visitor saw during an afternoon walk a very old monk cutting the grass; he asked the abbot who was equally hard working and also not very young anymore: "When can you finally take your retirement and enjoy your well-deserved rest?" The abbot pointed to the monastic cemetery down the road: "When they lay us down over there."

Work: Necessary Evil or Necessary Good?

Otiositas inimica est animae: "idleness is the enemy of the soul." Thus Benedict begins chapter 48 of his Rule that regulates daily work as well as the daily spiritual reading of the monk, just as it provides in the earlier chapters the order of daily communal choral prayers. With that, all three domains are named that might be indicated as the "central tasks" of a monastery: praying, working, and reading. The fourth domain of the monastic day, which is also regulated but is not active by nature, is most certainly an important domain, that of rest (in the afternoon and at night) and the so-called silence of night after Compline. Moreover, there is the equally important domain of the common meals. A separate chapter is dedicated to another central task, namely, the receiving of guests.

Benedict develops this topic in this forty-eighth chapter and elsewhere in his Rule, a small and mostly implicit theology of work. He was probably inspired by Augustine and others, who had written about this earlier, more expansively, more explicitly, and in a more theological manner. Yet we associate the daily cultivation of work with communities that follow Benedict's Rule rather than with the different offshoots of the Augustinian family. There are good reasons for this. Benedictines, and the Cistercians and Trappists, who originated through reforms in the Benedictine Order, live and work mostly in rural areas and have brought large areas under cultivation. Augustinians and Dominicans were, from the beginning, mostly communities that lived in the city. Their work was of a different nature; for example, preaching. *Ora et labora* (pray and work) is therefore a motto traditionally bound up with Benedictine life. It is a motto that easily misleads. To begin with, it does not occur in the Rule but is dated many centuries later. More in the spirit of the Rule, the motto should be *ora et labora et lege* (pray, work, and read). Moreover, it suggests a "contiguous" existence of domains (which is, of course, also the case chronologically in the order of the day) while, on a deeper level, it is about life of one piece, in which praying, working, and reading (and even recreation and rest) are done from the same basic attitude. That is expressed beautifully in another motto that does occur in the Rule: *ut in omnibus glorificetur Deus*—that God may be glorified in everything. This saying was borrowed from the First Letter of Peter (1 Pet 4:11), which closes the fifty-seventh chapter, dealing with the workers of the monastery, their products, and their prices. The context of production, buying, and selling is also one in which God may be glorified—or not, of course. This motto is found in early times already in monastic documents, in decorations, and above monastery portals, often abbreviated as I.O.G.D. Apparently, it was deemed important as well as characteristic. It expresses in a striking manner that everything may be sanctified, that everything in a monastic day merits care and attention: from the singing of psalms to peeling potatoes, from the preparation of sermons to cleaning toilets, from the solemn liturgy to listening to a CD during recreation with a few fellow brothers, from the writing of an important letter to the municipality where the congregation is situated, to a relaxed conversation with a guest during the afternoon walk.

Benedict begins chapter 48 about work and (spiritual) reading with an obviously pragmatic and "negative" reason: idleness is not good for the monk. Boredom arises and may change into sourness and depression: the *acedia* of listlessness. Here, of course, a spiritual dimension is also present: since antiquity, work has been seen as a medicine against *acedia*. This is, of course, also the case outside the monastery. Many know the experience that feelings of listlessness automatically recede when you have set yourself to a task; such feelings diminish proportionately as you busy yourself with a task more intensively and more persistently. On the other hand, listlessness only increases if you keep postponing the real work or replace it with empty pseudo-activities.

Elsewhere Benedict also mentions an obvious positive and pragmatic argument to give work a serious place in the monastic day; the general activities keep the monastic organization moving; the work of the artisans and the work on the land contribute to the maintenance of the life of the community. But as idleness drains the drive, the spirit and the *pneuma*, and makes you lose your spiritual way, so work can "pneumatize" you and be an impulse on your spiritual way. This thought is already implicit in the opening words of chapter 48: if idleness is the enemy of your soul, then work is its friend. The quality of my work and the condition of my soul are intimately connected. My work expresses how my soul is faring. That is also true outside the monastery. Even with small housekeeping tasks—peeling potatoes, putting away the washed dishes, repairing a leaky tire—we experience that an aggressive, tense, or poorly concentrated mind produces different results than when a person is calm, attentive, and balanced. That would not be any different in the managing of a company, the performing of cardiac surgery, or in carrying out political responsibility. On the other hand, your *pneuma-level* (your soul force) rises when you consciously and in a disciplined manner daily apply yourself to activities that feed you: solid reading, cultivating the study of music, keeping up your herb garden.

Here is another general spiritual dimension of work: at work as part of your spiritual way, you constantly meet yourself, others, and God, says Anselm Grün, economist of a large monastic community. In your work also you are essentially "in God's service." The economist-monk needs to be "godly" in the investing, in the consultation with fellow workers, and in the contact with local authority. Being godly is not an attitude that must exclusively be cultivated in a monastic chapel.

Benedict's view of work and its spiritual importance stands in sharp contrast with the late ancient spirit of the age. *Everyone* works in the monastery: the patrician who has entered, the intelligent scholar and rhetorician, the few priests who need the abbey (during Benedict's time, the monastery was a *lay* community; Benedict, as far as we know, was not a priest), the former slave, and the abbot, for he is also *subject to the Rule*. No one is excepted from the general tasks: everyone contributes according to his *capacities*. The last part occurs almost as a refrain: the abbot must carefully see to it that no one is overloaded (himself included!), but also that no one is "under-loaded." Moreover, work is not to be isolated from the rest of community life; neither is it to be seen as a primary entity. It contributes to good housekeeping (economy), but it is not the be-all and end-all of that housekeeping.

In the ancient world, a purely contemplative life was a high ideal, being free of obligations, a worthy relaxed life: *otium cum dignitate* (in a more hedonist form called "Feeling of a Swiss life"). Work was a concern for slaves and storekeepers, and not more than a necessary "evil." For Benedict, work is indeed necessary, but only as a necessary *good*, a *bonum*. Work does the monk good and is valuable: *labor cum dignitate*.

Once again, this has a broader significance: all of us prosper best if we are active (together) at regular times; we grow through others. Particularly when we enjoy being at work, really with the things that occupy us (that is the literary meaning of *inter-esse*), we know the experience that has recently been labeled "flow." It is flowing almost by itself, but that apparent flowing by itself is the result of a cultivated, built-up "difference in pressure," a disciplined "building up of the *pneuma*." The Benedictine flow is related to this; the work is fed by silence, choral prayers, reading, and rest—elements that flow together into the order of the day. With many of these things attention and concentration are important, but also a relaxed attitude. Perhaps that is the monastic variant of the ancient *otium*: not being free *from* work and an assigned structured division of time but being free *in* the context of work, prayer, reading, and rest.

Benedictine Attitudes to Work

The Benedictine basic attitudes pertain to *all* aspects of monastic life—thus, also to work. They are summarized in the three promises the monk expresses with his profession (the solemn incorporation into the community): the promises mentioned above of *stabilitas*, *conversio morum*, and *obedientia*. We repeat them here once more and relate them to daily work.

Stabilitas represents persistence and sticking with it, with what the situation and your fellow brother ask of you, even when it is not yet going too well, and the result is disappointing, and the end of the job lies in the distant future. Negatively formulated, *stabilitas* is the art of not running away from the things and the people to whom you have given your "yes," to whom you have committed yourself. There are many subtle forms of running away without physically leaving your place. Daydreaming, "postponement behavior," pseudo-activity, "nipping away" at something other than what you should be busy with—you can spend an entire day in your workplace without doing anything and still come home dog tired from the "nipping at" fake jobs. Modern communication technology offers generous opportunities "to run away" and can result in a conflicted attitude toward *stabilitas*. To use a German word, *stabilitas* means *Dranbleiben*. *Dranbleiben* demands concentration, perseverance, not being diverted by outside stimuli that are external to what is asked of you. On the other hand, *Dranbleiben* is not to be glued to your work or completely being stuck with it. You should be able to let go precisely when that is asked of you. It is about both concentrating and also being relaxed with the activity. *Stabilitas* and *inter-esse* thus support each other.

Dranbleiben is still "neutral" relative to its moral quality: a lung transplant and a well-planned and well-executed bank robbery both demand persistence and concentration. *Stabilitas* needs to be coupled with a striving for a positive outcome. That is expressed in the monastic attitude of *conversio morum* (in some sources it is also called *conversatio morum*). This is about the daily attention for improved quality in our style of living and working. With *conversio* (conversion, turnabout) we very quickly think of drastic experiences that may turn our life upside down. Such experiences do occur (sometimes), but these are not oriented to *conversio morum*. It is rather about being persistent in our daily search for, and particularly of, all those little possibilities we might call micro-conversion: being a little less irritated when you pick up the phone, being a bit more courteous and understanding toward your fellow brother who now and then makes more mistakes with the singing of psalms than you do, reading two beautiful poems before going to sleep instead of flipping the television channels, typing the performance report—in such a report every word counts!—and not letting your attention be diverted by your weekend plans or your concern about what a colleague said to you the day before. I mentioned earlier a brother who worked for a long time in the United States who once described the *conversio morum* as the daily turnaround from *trash* to *treasures*. There is always some junk to be disposed of in your life and work. Chances of being oriented toward giving small quality impulses to your life and work always present themselves.

Obedientia or obedience has to do with very attentive listening. The word is derived from *ob-audire*, which means a strengthened listening. *Obedientia* dovetails with the first and most important word of the Rule of Benedict: *ausculta* or *obsculta*—listen!

"Listen, my son and incline the ear of your heart!"—this is how the Rule begins. This is about perceptive and keen listening, as a physician "listens" to a patient. It is to hear what is going on, to judge what the situation is, and then to act as that situation demands of you. It is a listening directed to the act. It is also listening that truly needs to adapt to the things presented, to be with them, to hear well what is demanded. That "inclining the ear of your heart" is to genuinely examine what is asked of you: your supervisor, your "superior" (who can also be a student of yours; the Benedictine attitude implies that you may need to bow for everything and everyone, and thus may view everything and everyone as something or someone higher, something or someone whom you esteem highly and want to keep high), your fellow brother, a guest, a class, a situation, an entire enterprise. No rigid discipline fits the Benedictine obedience (since it is not "from the heart") and no internal resistance either. Obedience has to do with answering each other, an alert and affectionate listening to what is asked of you and adequately react to it as well, to respond, to react responsibly.

Daily work is also an exercise in humility—an important Benedictine virtue that has already been referred to. To do your work from an attitude of humility is literally "ex-centric." The center toward which you are directed lies outside you—that student, that problem, a dysfunctional apparatus, a stagnating organization, your "inferior" with whom you as the leader conduct a performance conversation. This attitude prevents the loss of energy and quality as a result of I-targeted double meanings (and thus not toward the work or toward the other), such as perfectionism, inflating of the ego, ambition, and competition with fellow workers.

To the lowliness or humility also belong a realistic self-image (the CEO is but a little man) and a realistic view of what is possible and impossible in a given situation. Humility makes it possible to view realistically such matters that do not succeed well, and to view frustrations realistically. That provides internal freedom and teaches us to let go.

Humility is also a fitting attitude in handling equipment and other things in the monastery. Just like you, these things are also in the service of the community. As such they merit respect, they deserve to be held "high." Benedict offers a creation spirituality on a micro-level; he keeps emphasizing the importance of a careful dealing with whom and what is entrusted to you. This is how you contribute positively to your environment. Humility is a question of both material and social ecology.

This attitude of humility is likely to be very contrary to our present culture of autonomy, success, exaggeration, brightening up, and self-satisfied mission statements, when all strive to belong to the top. Yet it is not at all excluded that our life together would measurably cheer up if the virtue of humility were practiced and cultivated somewhat more intensively.

Pressure of Work

In gatherings with leaders I have guided, gatherings in which the relationship between spirituality and leadership was central, when people introduced themselves and told something about their motivation to participate, the most frequent keyword was "hectic" or a synonym.

Many in our society, not in the least those who bear responsibility, have the feeling that they do not lead a good life. Nevertheless, they do not manage to step out of the vicious circle of their overload, as Anselm Grün often remarks in his days of reflection with leaders. Many among them feel permanently overloaded and exhausted. Exhaustion, claims Grün, always has two causes: you are not able to pace yourself, you cross the boundary; and/or you draw from murky sources that drain extra energy, such as perfectionism, ambition, the craving to satisfy all expectations, and to be loved by everyone. These desires are not realistic and do not mesh with an attitude of humility. The practice of humility might well be the best medicine against overload and exhaustion.

In my own (university) surroundings I often note that the people from whom renewal and creativity are expected are the same people who are permanently overloaded (particularly with tasks that are at odds with quiet, concentrated study and free investigation, which does not have to be successful by the day after tomorrow). They feel they are under pressure. A striking aphorism by Cornelis Verhoeven states that this is not fruitful: "Under pressure everything becomes flat." The pressure of performance is a contradiction in this field. Creativity, the acknowledgment of new ideas, demands precisely a certain "low pressure": free space, sometimes daring to check out a dead-end road (often one meets something interesting); to take a day off and visit a museum when things get stuck; to dare to follow your intuition for something that only much later might produce fruit—none of these mesh with a quick settling of accounts whose goal is quick and useful success. Yet the history of science abundantly shows that creativity and renewal—thus, true success and real fruit—succeed best under the preconditions of tenacious patience, the worriless walking of side paths, and the free following of what captivates you.

At the same time I often note an "under-loading" of those from whom creativity and renewal is expected in the future. In terms of both time (contact hours and real study time) and content, many types of education have suffered from an almost unbearable lightness. The success of special programs (*honors programs*, for example) is notable when they offer students something extra, often of more demanding and interdisciplinary material. "This is why I really came to the university," I heard a student say. When we asked further, it appeared that the entire group felt the same way.

Benedict is opposed to overloading, but he is also against "under-loading." Monks must not live under the pressure of overloading or being driven by it, as we read in chapter 48 quoted above, which is about work and reading.

Driving and bustle do not fit in monastic life, and actually not in a good community either. Driving and bustle have something to do with violence. The Trappist Thomas Merton suggests in this connection, "The rush and the pressure of modern life are a form, perhaps the most common form, of its innate violence."

What helps in the monastery is a healthy tension between contemplation and activity, between breathing in and out—it is the daily order. The monastic bell indicates that it is time for the midday prayers and that you therefore need to shut off the word processor or put your lawnmower in the barn. After the meal and the afternoon recreation, the bell rings again: end of the recreation, time to continue with the work. Etcetera, day in, day out. The monastic order of the day helps to exercise virtue in reality and at the same time to begin with the task that lies before you—and not with the behavior of postponement and pseudo-activity, maintaining the appearance that you are busy and active. One also cultivates virtue in dropping the work pronto when it is time for prayer or spiritual reading, and forgoing to meet or do the accounting when you are to gather with your brothers and sing the psalms in the choir. That is how you exercise the right attitude during the period "between two bells": really being with things, *Dranbleiben*, letting no energy and no quality to be drained by things that do not belong in their slot of time.

When it works, the attitude of the monk during the monastic day is relaxed and dignified. The monastic day teaches the art of being in a "resigned" spirit, to give everything its time, also a break. A busily occupied day can then be without stress.

Benedict underscores the importance of recreation and meditation. With the translation of Benedictine spirituality into manners of life and work outside the monastery, we need to be careful that we do not "manage" recreation too efficiently. That calls forth a specter of the manager who also wishes to optimally utilize family time, sports, and meditation. He who wishes to "manage" time permanently, Anselm Grün claims in this connection, makes time into an opponent and does experience it thus, and not as a daily gift.

Another instrument for preventing overloading of monks is an attentive awareness when someone needs help. There are numerous places in the Rule where Benedict brings this up. When the work of the economist or other functionaries, from prior to porter and from guestmaster to cook, threatens to become too great, the abbot sees to it that help will arrive. That is also true, however, and in particular, for the abbot himself. For all areas of work and tasks in the monastery the basic rule applies: those who need help will also receive it—a regularly returning refrain in several chapters. Outside the monastery, this also appears to me as a basic rule for a social ecology and for lasting enterprise. *Sustainability* has also to do with what your people can bear.

No one in the monastery may be overburdened, and no one should be "under-loaded." "The abbot must regulate everything with a sense of rhythm so that the weaker brothers will not shrink back from heavy tasks, but that something remains for the strong to reach for," we read in the Rule. Those who need help will receive it. Those who are free should stand ready for any task.

Blessed Work: A Question of the Right Word

In work situations, in the monastery and elsewhere, communication is going on. Assignments are given, there is consultation about work, reports are given, reactions are shared.

Listening with the ear of the heart is an essential precondition for fruitful work. But also speaking the right word in the right manner is essential. In another chapter we will return to this theme. A few comments may be offered for clarification here.

Blessed and fruitful work is a question of speaking "well" and listening with the heart. Speaking well in Latin is *bene-dicere*, which may also mean "to bless," obviously mutually related mean-ings. *Male-dicere* is saying bad words, or perhaps good words said in a wrong manner. There are leaders who are capable of delivering an unpleasant message in such a good manner that the hearer, in trust and with engagement, tries to make the best of it. Others succeed in delivering even a good message in a wrong manner so that no one has confidence in it, while it stagnates the matter in question, for example, by stalling, silent sabotage, or grumbling.

Benedict judges grumbling to be the most serious sin in the monastery. Twelve times he warns emphatically against *murmu-ratio*, and particularly that the leaders should not give occasion to *murmuratio*. This is not about occasionally venting your heart, or that perhaps you not tell your abbot (in a fitting manner, of course) that a certain task is too heavy for you. *Murmuratio* concerns poisonous grumbling or grousing. Such grumbling acts as slowly working poison in the community. Grumblers look for company and strengthen one another. Grumbling leads to undesirable spiritual fission that sickens the community. But there is also an antidote, the cheerful, well-spoken good word. The good word can work as balm for the soul; it is just like grumbling, but in a positive manner; it is contagious and results in a positive spiritual cell division. The cheerful, well-spoken, good word can help you stand upright and with good courage tackle a very heavy or even an impossible assignment. Just as bad words have a cascade of negative results, hurt people, sicken relationships, drain away life and the *pneuma*, so good words spoken in the right manner have a wholesome result: they heal, generate life, and bless.

The Benedictine "minding your words" is, of course, of broader application. Many complaints at work and a good deal of absence due to sickness appear to be related to wrong or wrongly spoken words (or unspoken words) of those who give leadership. This fact of experience has a complement: the cultivation of the *bene-dicere* in communication at work leads to the reduction of costs and more fruitful work.

Benedictine work, which, of course, non-Benedictines may follow, is simply more economical. It promotes good housekeeping.

References for Chapter 4

Derkse, Wil. *The Rule of Benedict for Beginners: Spirituality for Daily Life*. Collegeville, MN: Liturgical Press, 2004.

Grün, Anselm, OSB. *Leben und Beruf. Eine spirituelle Herausforderung*. Münsterschwarzach, Germany: Vier Türme-Verlag, 2005.

Puzicha, Michaela, OSB. *Kommentar zum Benediktusregel*. Erzabtei Sankt Ottilien: EOS Verlag, 2002.

————. *Benedikt von Nursia begegnen*. Augsburg, Germany: Sankt Ulrich Verlag, 2004.

Schmidbauer, Wolfgang. *Dranbleiben—die gelassene Art, Ziele zu erreichen*. Freiburg, Germany: Herder, 2002.

West, Norvene. *Friend of the Soul: A Benedictine Spirituality of Work*. Boston: Cowley, 1997.

5

The Daily Study:
In Contact with Nurturing Sources

Benedict discusses daily study in the same chapter as daily labor (48). Apparently he saw it as two sides of the same coin. Every day work is done, and every day study is done, and indeed during the full course of monastic life, as long as one is not plagued by physical limitations or obstacles; but even then one searches for accommodated forms of work and study. The monk is never finished working and never finished studying. That sounds like a heavy and lifelong yoke to bear, as a tough daily penance to keep up. But as we learned in the previous chapter, Benedict did not judge work a necessary evil but a "necessary good." Work is good for the soul of the monk and for the soul of the community. This also applies to daily study; it enlarges and liberates the soul. It concerns related and complementary aspects of monastic life. In work, it may be said, the monk is outwardly active, but related to an internal attitude of the soul. In study the monk is internally receptive and in a sense also active, but in relationship with external preconditions: silence and absence of other external stimuli, the right physical posture, a suitable place for study, and a nurturing text. In the daily liturgy the external and internal meet one another optimally. Thus, study is an essential part of the dynamic balance of the monastic day and monastic life. This is valid for everyone, not only for the "intellectuals" among the brothers.

Our concept of "study" comes from the Latin word *studere*. Benedict uses the word not in chapter 48 but in chapter 42 about the silence after Compline (the celebration that closes the day): "At every point of time the monks need to exercise silence [*silentium debent studere monachi*], but particularly during the hours of the night." *Studere* means here the diligent application, the serious cultivation of, in this case, "being silent." One might suggest that monastic life as a whole is an opportunity for *studere*, the diligent application and the serious cultivation of everything: the choral prayers, hospitality, mutual brotherliness, silence, the acceptance of guests, daily work, and thus also the daily *lectio divina*. For this is what Benedict calls the daily "study." And there is solid reading to be done daily; the Rule says that one should "make oneself free" for *lectio* for about two hours (the length differs in summer and winter). During the fasts, extra study time is added, and on Sunday all make themselves "free" for *lectio* outside the liturgical times, apart from those who take a turn for the daily tasks in the house.

This "making free" may be taken literally: Benedict often uses the word *vacare*, which is the origin of our word "vacation," in the verses about study. Abbot Guillaume Jedrzejczak of Katsberg notes in his commentary on this chapter that *vacare* is a conscious creating of emptiness and space in which the spirit and the heart are freed from other cares, as if the daily cares were left behind at the door of the monastic cell or of the study room. In the space that has thus been vacated, the good Word of God (that may speak in many texts) can be listened to, taken up, internalized, and "answered." The fast, according to Abbot Guillaume, might therefore be seen as the "great vacation" of the monk, because he might make himself even freer for *lectio*, "so that the symphony of the Scriptures begins to sing in him." In this light, one might even see the entire monastic life as freeing oneself for God: in prayer, in work, in study, in hospitality, in mutual respect, in recreation, and so in everything listening to and answering God's voice. The motto of the Saint Adelbertus Abbey of Egmond is, therefore, *Deo vacare*. One of the brothers there told me once that the people of the surrounding village freely translate this: "Those boys there always have vacation." In a profound sense that is indeed the case.

Lectio: Reading to Live

Reading in the Benedictine tradition is not intended primarily to inform oneself and to acquire knowledge—even though such information may be "taken along" on the way and is sometimes needed to acquire a good understanding of the texts. The reading of texts is intended to *live* out of them. This is about sources you may *draw from*, as the life-supporting water of which Psalm 1 speaks, and where the man who wishes to gain growth needs to put down his roots, so that, in that place, God's nurturing Word might daily penetrate him. Reading does not primarily have a cognitive but rather an existential goal; it is not so much about knowing more, but to gain more life. Abbot Christopher Jamison points out that the reader is not primary with *lectio divina*, but rather with the text and with the one who speaks in it. Humility is again suitable in *lectio*: "Avoid laying your questions on the text but let the text question *you*."

In monastic life, the first sentence of the Prologue is applied; it is pointed, "auscultating" reading in which the text is, as it were, carefully listened to with a stethoscope in order to hear what it has to say to me and to what it calls me. That implies slow and repeated reading. With a hasty, diagonal-like move through a text you can certainly pick up some information, but the words will not reach your heart. For just as in that first sentence, the *inclinatio cordis* is important here: it is reading with an affectionate heart. Surely, in the early monastic period, *lectio divina* was also intended to memorize important texts, or, as the English language puts it, almost Benedictine, *by heart*. Because our hearts are so different, the texts that might nurture us and where we might exercise the *inclinatio cordis* will differ. Benedict must surely have been aware of this; in the chapter about work and study he prescribes that on the first day of Lent, the "great reading vacation," every monk must be given his own "Lenten book" (he probably meant a Bible book), apparently selected for this person, that he is to read from beginning to end.

With *lectio* the very different nature and inclination of the brothers and sisters needs to be borne in mind. I saw this beautifully illustrated in what my beloved fellow brother Henri Boelaars, OSB, (1912–2001) told me. As a young artist in 1929 he entered the Saint Paulus Abbey in Oosterhout from which the Saint Willibrord's Abbey was later founded, of which he became one of the builders. Because of a serious hearing disturbance he could not pursue philosophical and theological studies to prepare himself for a life that was then called that of a "choir monk" and the priesthood that was often connected with it. Thus, he was trained as a "lay brother" (Benedict himself did not know this distinction, likely because he was not a priest but a layman), with a suitable training program. The prayers of the Hours (the Our Father and the *Ave Maria*) and the *lectio* of the lay brothers were, at the time, cultivated at a "lower" level than those of the choir monks. Thanks to the alert priest who was the "brother master," and who fortunately had noticed the sharp and alert artist's eye of Brother Henri, he assigned him the biography of Hildegard of Bingen (ca. 1098–1179) for *lectio*. This was soon followed by the *Scivias* ("Know your ways") that Hildegard wrote, which were provided with beautiful but puzzling page illuminations. This became the point of departure for Brother Henri for more than sixty years of meditative contact with the texts and particularly with the illuminations of Hildegard's vision book, *Scivias*. Daily he dedicated at least a half hour to these texts and what goes along with them; during the first decades he was accompanied by involved fellow brothers. His goal was not to become a scholar in this area but to feed himself with it. This almost lifelong "project" also became for Brother Henri a kind of lifeline in his monastic life. It gave him a footing and stability in difficult and chaotic periods, and extra joy in his advanced age when his love for Hildegard was gradually shared in a broader circle of academics and others. At the end of his life, when he lay in a coma because of a serious illness, he had his own "visions" that he shared in the hospital with the exceptionally involved and caring companion in the abbey who assisted him to the end of his life. He said that he had *seen* something, with the directness of St. Paul and Teresa of Avila, a seeing different than the arts he had studied all during his life, without means or *center*, but directly. He had also seen that Hildegard had been but a *medium* on the road to this directness.

I suspect that people outside a monastery can also profit from a "project" like that of Brother Henri—cultivating a domain of attention as a kind of refuge in the midst of your other cares, on which you are concentrating daily, if only for a half hour. You can grow in it, and finally grow so much beyond it that you realize your "project" has a destiny that is without boundary.

The example of Brother Henri gives an indication of what was and is read during the time of *lectio divina*. Benedict himself indicates several sources. First, all the books of the Bible, but also for him relatively recent and contemporary writings, such as the works of John Cassian, the *Sayings* of the Fathers, and the Rule of Basil. The content of his Rule makes us suspect that Benedict's library also contained works of Jerome, Ambrose, and Augustine. But the readers' "search for God" did not hesitate to draw from other sources than those an earlier generation might label as "pious literature." The Benedictine Jean Leclercq, who wrote an impressive book about monastic "study," concludes that monks and nuns attentively read the Scriptures and, of course, the church fathers, but also ancient "pagan" literature. Saint Boniface remarked already during the eighth century that a good understanding of the subtleties of the Holy Scriptures may be promoted by a good familiarity with the "grammar" and content of ancient writings. Leclercq claims that these writings were, of course, not read by themselves because they were helpful for a better understanding of religious texts, but because monks and nuns found them beautiful and enjoyed reading them. These texts developed their taste, taught them subtle literary forms, and brought them into contact with perceptive forms of moral sensibility. The discovery then quickly followed that one can learn from reading very different traditions and contexts.

This is precisely the current practice of *lectio divina*: brothers and sisters seek for sources that are suitable for them, a process by which, when it is good, the superior and others can offer orientation, and they do that quite seriously.

Lectio outside the Monastery Walls

The philosopher of culture George Steiner in his *Lessons of the Masters* (2003) issues a fervent plea for the high calling (and dangerous risks) of intensive contact between master and student. One of the important forms of this contact he finds in simply sitting down with a book in which a "master" is speaking. The silence and sustained attention of the concentrating reader is a great virtue, whereby "virtue" is not seen as a form of courage, but like classical tradition sees virtue, as a gradually acquired attitude of excellence. The masters whom Steiner admires are themselves also solid readers. One might say that solid reading is the precondition for one's own (possibly quite modest and unnoticed) mastership. In a culture of overwhelming bombardment of rapidly changing and successive communication in sharp images and often loud music, a plea for solid reading and sitting down with a book for a long time seems a lost cause.

In an interview that George Steiner gave in *Le magazine littéraire* about the French translation of his book about masters and students,[10] he pointed to signals in society that ought to be taken seriously, and from which appear that the longing for reading is vital at all times and in all cultures. Steiner, who was asked to label himself in this interview as *maître à lire* (reading master), points, for example, to the remarkable fact that recently more than a billion substantial books were sold worldwide, written by a single author. This is J. K. Rowling, the author of the *Harry Potter* series:

> Chinese children stand in line at night to acquire volumes 3 and 4, very English books, based on boarding school life in British *public schools*, with a complex sentence structure and using a rich, rather old fashioned vocabulary. The entire planet devours these books. Children ask their parents to turn off the television so that they can read and reread *Harry Potter* undisturbed.

This phenomenon is more than the result of an accompanying media campaign, Steiner claims, for with advertising alone you do not reach hundreds of millions of people, from Chinese to Inuit, to the point that they will read large and complex books. With the best of preconditions you might persuade the children to start reading the *Odyssey*. But precisely these preconditions are threatened in an educational system of small, preferably "jazzed up" little tasks, a lessening of contact hours between master and pupil, and (in the Netherlands at any rate) a notable reduction of "book lists" that might encourage children to come into contact with the masters of our culture. This risky development, says Steiner, presents itself in many cultural domains: "When we do not teach children to develop the capacity to sit down calmly and quietly with a text, a musical piece or a painting, we may expect a profound crisis in western culture."

It becomes ever more difficult to value highly the important essential values, such as that of silence and the art of the power of discretion; but they are worth fighting for to keep them alive.

This is precisely what monastic reading aims at, but this may also be cultivated outside the monastery walls, bringing forth fruits.

Michael Casey, the Trappist, once illustrated the value of reading by pointing "to the negative effects of not reading on the life of the one who gives in to doing nothing or just talking."

Instead of the "internal traveling" that solid reading offers us, our internal life will be filled by other sources, mostly by the mass media. "If it is true that listlessness is a dominant characteristic of contemporary Western culture, then the most obvious symptom of it must be the flight from boredom and the unceasing thirst for excitement and amusement." Michael Casey claims that we might do well to thoroughly review our attitude toward the mass media:

> The mass media constantly inundate our critical thoughts, opinions are postulated as facts, a good impression is valued higher than truth and with a *spin* everything can have a meaning which the commentator aims at. I do not doubt that a continual confrontation with this will eventually have a degenerating effect on the spirit.

The continual impact of television and the internet does not only devour time that we could spend better, but we also allow things to enter our soul that create damage. It is a very relevant question to ask what we allow to enter: *trash* or *treasures*? The first had better be cleared out; the second is precisely the goal of solid reading that the monastic tradition finds important and that can also be fruitful outside the monastery.

The decision to keep *trash* outside and to allow *treasures* to enter works in a liberating manner in a double respect, claims Michael Casey: it frees you from the manipulation of the mass media while it frees you in silence to establish contact with valuable sources that are of benefit.

In one of his books Michael Casey has further worked out the importance of solid reading and also the contrast of it with our culture.[11] He calls reading a *cool* medium, unlike television and the internet, which are *hot*. What does he mean by this? With reading we have the possibility to stop, to take a step back, and to think about what we have read. We may also compare our reading with what we have met in other sources. We might bring our reading experiences into contact with what we have read elsewhere and reflect on both domains. By definition, when we read we are "critical," which, according to its Greek roots, has to do with holding something to the light while examining it. Television, the internet, and other media are different by nature; they are *hot*. They immediately stimulate our emotions through all sorts of entries of which we are not even conscious, by cleverly chosen camera angles, input of irrelevant graphic and musical elements, "editing," and the omission of nuances. In our viewing we are almost naturally "uncritical"; "it offers food for the soul that needs to be swallowed instead of ruminated."

These objections refer particularly to the form, apart from the content and nature of what we swallow and do not ruminate. The content is often an explosion of trivialities. On the other hand, the monastic daily reading is targeted precisely on the nontrivial. Daily contact with triviality disintegrates and withers the soul. Daily contact with sources of value creates coherence (German, *Sammlung*) and makes the soul grow. One might say that someone who likes the *joie de vivre* might better end his day with a quiet and concentrated reading of a few beautiful poems than carelessly viewing quickly jumping images while switching from one channel to the next. It is not difficult to see the qualitative difference between these two attitudes optically and expressively. Someone who has slumped in his chair and lets one program after another flash by does not offer an uplifting view, while the view of someone who is studying or otherwise absorbed in literature is alluring and full of beauty.[12] There are, not surprisingly, many paintings in which such "beautiful reading" is pictured. For, says Michael Casey, "reading well-practiced is a way to the heart."

The sons and daughters of Benedict have been book lovers for almost fifteen hundred years, and they have good reason for this. They know that solid reading is an essential element of a "blessed life."

6

Benedictine Hospitality

In his Rule, Benedict apparently assumes that a monastery will never be without guests. A separate chapter (53) is dedicated to the reception of guests. In order not to disturb the brothers when unexpected guests check in (and there will be no lack of those, according to verse 16), the guests and the abbot (who is to welcome them) need to have their own kitchen. In chapter 56 (about the abbot's table), it is underscored once more that the abbot should always eat with the guests and the pilgrims. If there are but a few guests, he may invite a few brothers to his table.

In practice, these chapters of the Rule (and many others as well) are interpreted with some flexibility. Today's guests (and monks) would feel quite awkward if, after their ringing, the abbot and the entire community should rush to meet them (53.2, 3), exchange a kiss of peace with them (53.4, 5), and both at their arrival and departure demonstrate humility by lying prostrate on the earth (53.7). Abbot Guillaume of Katsberg tells us in his commentary on the Rule that he is very happy with the fact that he has been able to delegate the joint meal with the guests to brothers who are better suited for this contact than he is.

There are also monastic communities that for a few weeks annually accept no guests, for example, during retreats of the community, sometimes even with the express intent to be able afterward to be cordially and fully hospitable. Other communities, such as the beautifully located abbey of *La Pierre-qui-vire* in the wooded French Morvan, on their part have chosen to view the receiving of guests as their primary "labor" and have recently invested generously in a new building in addition to their already large guest house.[13] In our area, the Trappist abbey of Zundert has done the same.[14]

Even so, for almost fifteen hundred years in monasteries that follow the Rule of Benedict, hospitality belongs to one of the main tasks, in addition to several daily gatherings for the choral prayers (the Hours), spiritual reading and the forms of study, work of all sorts, the common meal(s), and the maintaining of the nightly silence.

Accepting Like the Lord Himself

The different ways hospitality is designed in monasteries are based on the same basic attitude. This basic attitude is "grafted" on chapter 53, mentioned above, of the Rule of Benedict and is strikingly expressed in the first sentence: "All guests must be received like Christ himself, for he will say: 'I was a stranger and you took me in.'" This is indeed rather to be *taken in* than to be received. Hospitality goes deeper than only offering shelter and care. The Lord (and any guest may be the Lord) is taken in among his pupils—a remembrance of the joy of Easter. Old rabbis used to say that hospitality is a form of worship. Another two verses of this chapter relate hospitality to meeting Christ. By greeting him with homage "we must pray to Christ as he is also received in him" (53.7). And: "Particularly when taking in poor and strangers the greatest care must be expended, because Christ is more particularly received in them" (53.7). Benedict delicately adds that the "rich" among the guests (in whom, of course, the Lord must be seen also) will be treated with awe and respect. This is not a superfluous remark, however; many a superior will now and then have to guard that, in the guest quarters, the appointed brothers and sisters (and even more the members *not* appointed by the community) particularly create pleasure in too intensive a contact with "particular" guests.

The manner in which the taking in of guests happens is described in this chapter in the Rule. It contains a combination of humanity, geniality, and humility (as we saw earlier—the courage to *serve*), apart from sympathy, feeling of status—this attitude is fitting toward *every* guest. For every guest may be the Lord, "even when she has her nose pierced," as I heard a brother say once. Not without ambiguous humor, Brother Benet Tvedten of Blue Cloud Abbey comments in this connection, "Benedict says that we must see Christ in our guests. And we always hope that they can see him in us."

It is a biblical tradition that guests are seen as messengers of God, and indeed sometimes as the Lord himself. Abbot Guillaume Jedrzejczak of Katsberg underscores in this connection, following the footsteps of Benedict, that a guest is not so much someone who asks something from us (shelter, food, attention) but someone who comes to bring us something, to wit *misericordiam tuam* (53.14). The guest is a present, God's gracious gift.

These are beautiful words and thoughts. However, from quite a few guests to whom I speak on the telephone or who announce themselves through my mailbox, my first impression is that they especially want something from me. The (difficult) art is then to get beyond that and try to acknowledge to what extent they might be God's gracious gifts. Even if I, for serious reasons (such as the respect for my own boundaries), cannot be of service, it is fitting to let them know with respect and a good word. For, says Benedict, we need to approach the guest with humility (53.6) and "good care" (53.9). And we need to realize that we are all regular (and in a sense, constant) guests. Thus, a guest holds up a mirror in front of me.

Limits and Preconditions of Hospitality

Benedict also pays attention to the boundaries and preconditions of hospitality. The presence of guests may not cause disturbances in the monastic climate of attention, silence, and daily order. That is the reason that only the abbot and the guest brother(s) speak and meet with the guests, and if needed take care that there should be a separate kitchen for unexpected visitors—again, so that the order of the community should not be disturbed. In quite a few abbeys there are, moreover, arrangements about the *number* of guests that can be taken in, relating to the size of the community itself.

It is important that the guests and the monastic community should be suitably separated, in addition to forms of contact, involvement, and participation—a separate guesthouse or guest wing, areas in the monastery that are reserved for the community (the *clausura*), and a separate table for the guests in the refectory.

Benedict proposes to appoint a monk as "host" (if necessary with assistants) whose soul is fully permeated by the fear of God, related to the thought that every guest may be the *Lord*. His fear of God will naturally prompt his high esteem for the guest. That every guest thus should be held in high esteem appears in the chapter about the table of the abbot and the guests: the abbot always sits with guests and pilgrims at the table (56.1). He may therefore not hide behind the activities of his office or more important obligations, or only eat with the guests if they have a high social function or if they otherwise might be indicated as a "high visit." For Benedict every visit is a "high visit."

Separate and "specialized" brothers and sisters have the guest quarters under their guard, so that the life of the monastic community should not be disturbed and confused. In the first place, perhaps, this is because guests on their own initiative might produce unrest (it happens sometimes), and because internal processes of unrest might arise. An example is when monks see the guests as a vent to share things they had better discuss with their superior or among themselves. Or another reason might be because monks, on their own initiative, "pastorally" approach certain guests or else try to evangelize. Such processes are neither good for the souls of the monks nor for those of the guests.

However, the concern is always that the guest may truly be *accepted*, so that the climate of true hospitality is protected. Only then the guests may be offered something of value, because the guests enter the abbey or visit the guesthouse for that climate. Abbot Guillaume of Katsberg judges it important that guests truly experience that they are guests of an abbey and not in a beautifully situated bed-and-breakfast, a quiet hotel, or a rather Spartan-equipped youth hostel. This is why the monastic climate of prayer and silence must be guarded and cultivated. Thus, maximum justice is done to the desires of the guests themselves, that their stay may evoke something within themselves, as with the group of our students that stayed for a weekend in Saint Willibrord's Abbey.

I have experienced the importance of the presentation in a carefully cultivated monastic context with other groups. When I may be permitted to tell something about Benedictine attitudes in courses for leaders and employers, the location where these talks take place is often determined by pragmatic reasons: the area where people come from, a contract that someone already has with a conference center, or the possibilities of the speakers. Thus it can happen that I discuss approximately the same topics in a two-day gathering in a comfortable conference hotel with generous rooms, a minibar, and cable television, or in the former eighteenth-century monastery for Augustinian nuns at Soeterbeeck that is now furnished as a study center of our university, or in Saint Willibrord's Abbey. I have noticed that this immediately provides a boost in terms of sphere, impact, and appreciation. A quietly situated conference hotel offers a good climate for such gatherings, but even so there are many external stimuli. Consequently, one sees more people make telephone calls or send e-mail messages in their free hours than at Soeterbeeck or in the abbey. In the sober but beautiful spaces of Soeterbeeck, the subdued library, for example, and in the refectory that is used as a dining room, a different group climate is created. The fellow workers of the study center have managed to create a quiet and subdued climate. The somewhat modernized cells of the sisters that are used as guestrooms (without minibar and television, of course) invite guests to read something good before going to sleep rather than make some active telephone calls or work on the internet. In the morning I often see guests sitting quietly in the chapel (which is still used) before breakfast. When people remain in the retreat center of the abbey, certain important dimensions are added to the experience of the participants. In small details (such as the periodic ringing of the monastery bell, brothers they meet during their walks, or activity in and around the monastery), they notice that they are guests of a living monastic fellowship. They participate mostly on a voluntary basis in the prayers of the Hours, speak intensively as a group with one of the monks, and purchase books in the monastery store. As to small details, I observe the results: they go to bed earlier spontaneously, at the service of readings at 6:15 a.m. there is already a part of the group that participates, there is a notably economical use of cell telephones, and, just like with my students, I hear now and then some light humming in the corridors and in the garden.

The Porter

Another "host" has his own chapter, namely, the final chapter of Benedict's first edition of the Rule (66): the porter. This is the first person who meets the guest at the gate and thus also the first to welcome the guest in a climate of hospitality. The porter is also an important "filter" in the relationship between the "outside world" (which is surely not the evil, wicked outside world) and the monastic world of the community (that may not be viewed as Paradise either). This filter is important to do justice to whoever knocks, and do justice to the monastic climate beyond the gatehouse.

So that the guest does not need to wait too long, Benedict suggests that the porter have his cell near the gate. The manner of opening the door, to be available without tarrying, gratitude for the fact that the guest is present—all of these are expressed in the advice to answer the guest immediately after knocking with,

"Bless me" (*Benedicite*), or "Thanks be to God" (*Deo gratias*).
Benedict judges the function of the porter important; it must
therefore be entrusted to an older and wise monk. "Older" is
not necessarily intended chronologically; it has to do with spiritual maturity, as is expected from other monks who bear extra
responsibility in the community. Such maturity is, among other
things, the responsibility of the porter; he must be able to listen
and give a suitable answer. Listening and answering from the heart
express the center of Benedictine life. Benedict opens his Rule
with it. Thus also the porter. The guest may expect from him
a listening ear and a good answer. People who have experience
with the work of the hostess and the host in the guesthouse will
recognize the importance of a listening ear and also the capacity
for distinction to answer with the right word in a conversation—
whereby silence can sometimes be the most fitting and salutary
answer.

Benedict has a good feeling, as was mentioned earlier, for the
importance of good words, to say things well: *bene-dicere*, which
also means "to bless." The opposite is *male-dicere*, speak badly. A
special form of *male-dicere* is *murmuratio*, stubborn grumbling.
Benedict calls particularly those who bear extra responsibility to
prevent the occurrence of *murmuratio*. How so? By using good
words and saying things in a good manner, *benedicere*. This is true
for Benedictine hospitality: inclining the ear of your heart and
answering actively (as it says in the first sentence of the Rule) are
the attitudes the host and the hostess need to cultivate.

Hospitality differs (just like that of other central tasks) from
monastery to monastery. Trappists, male and female, and female
Benedictines often have separate guesthouses—guests eat separately. In most Benedictine monasteries the guest table is a part
of the monastic refectory. Sometimes the abbot eats at the same
table (in Egmond, for example). Sometimes only male guests are
welcome in this manner (Vaals, Doetinchem); sometimes one
sees guests of both sexes eat in the refectory (Egmond, Zeven-
kerken). Sometimes the concentration is on specific target groups,
which are offered their own programs (as in Münsterschwarzach,

Germany); sometimes hospitality consists of one guest sharing
as much as possible the life of the community—though in that
case there is, of course, also room for a conversation with one of
the monks, as in Saint Willibrord's Abbey.

My own abbey offers three forms of hospitality.[15] The first
was just mentioned—male guests who live for a few days, up to
a week, in a wing of the monastery and participate as much as
possible in monastic activities according to their inclination or
depending on the climate: the attendance and, if possible, participation in the singing of the Hours; personal study or reflection
in one's own cell; participating in the common meals; sometimes
also helping with practical activities in house or surrounding area.
In 2004 there were more than four hundred male guests.

The second form of hospitality of Saint Willibrord's Abbey
takes place in Hoeve Bethlehem, a silent center organized in
the former stables in the area of the abbey. Groups of men and
women are received here who mostly "bring along" their own
program (with their leaders), which is, however, in some way
related to the religious life and monastic spirituality. These guests
eat in their own dining room, though they are welcome to attend
the prayers of the Hours in the monastic church. In years past,
many hundreds of people, from students to business people,
stayed close to the community life, which gave their own program
a very different tone and atmosphere than when they had been
together in an "ordinary" conference center.

The third and the most approachable form of hospitality is
offered in the Guesthouse Castle Slangenburg. Most guests remain at least three days in the castle. Meals are taken in common; for the rest of the time, they organize the day as they wish,
though the order of the day enables the guests to participate in
the Hours and the celebration of the Eucharist in the abbey, an
opportunity that is taken advantage of by a good many of them.
Hostesses and hosts in large measure determine the climate of
the guesthouse. They welcome new guests, give structure to the
meals, are present with the pouring of coffee and tea, and are
available for personal conversations.

In addition to the "pastoral" tasks of the hostesses and hosts, for part of the week a pastor is present who also leads a weekly celebration of the Eucharist in the guesthouse. A second pastor, who is also an oblate of the abbey, concentrates on short lectures, introductions to the liturgy, and providing information on the monastic life in the abbey. Spiritual care occurs in good contact with the abbot of the abbey and with the administration of the Foundation Guesthouse Castle Slangenburg.

When I once spoke about Benedictine hospitality during a gathering of hostesses and hosts of Guesthouse Castle Slangenburg (I probably told them little that was new to them), one of the reactions came as a question about whether Benedict, in addition to all the "requirements" of the abbot, brother, porter, and community, also says something in his Rule about what may be expected of the *guest*. It would be strange if the Lord were first handed a packet of demands before he might enter! But Benedict was a realist. Between the rules, one notes that the guest may not disturb the good order of the monastic community. That comes first, so that the guest may be totally free. However, there is one place where he speaks more specifically about certain guests. Chapter 61 is about "strange" monks from elsewhere who wish to be guests of the monastery. Such people must indeed be accepted for as long as they wish, but under a few conditions: they must be content with the manner of life they meet in the monastery, and they are not allowed to cause unrest and confusion in the community, for example, by exaggerated demands. However, with Benedict the nuance is never lacking; if this guest with all humility and from genuine affinity offers well-founded critique or other comments, the abbot benefits by considering such comments. Perhaps the Lord sent this guest to the monastery precisely for this reason.

Benedictine Hospitality outside the Monastery

The oblate desires to give a fruitful place to the Benedictine attitudes in his or her own life context. Hospitality is part of that, both at home and on the job. When I am welcomed as a guest in the abbey, I note that a period of transition and acclimatizing is cultivated. This happens on both sides. I do not find it pleasant to arrive just before a service, having to rush to get my choir book to be on time in the chapel. Rather, I arrive with ample time before the service and enter the somewhat protected little portal before the gate to sit in a little pew, to catch my breath, and to let some tension drain out of my system. After that, I ring the bell. Because of the dimensions of the building, some time passes before the brother who serves as porter can open the door. After the greeting I am led to a parlor while the porter alerts the guest brother, who has already prepared for tea and coffee. We sit down together for a while and talk about how things are going in my home, at work, and in the community. Then I am taken to my room, put down my things, after which I go the monastic church to just sit down for a few minutes. Then I return to my cell to make my bed, to arrange my things, and put the ribbons in the right places in my choir book. When, after the first ringing of the bell, I sit down in the church to prepare myself for Vespers, then I am really there. Indeed, this is very different from when I, through circumstances, come driving in ten minutes before, which has also happened.

To receive guests at home occurs in a similar fashion. When they arrive, a simple process of acclimatization can occur in which guests can catch their breath and we can get used to each other. That should not be done in a hurried fashion. No one should be pushed into a chair, for perhaps he wishes to walk around a bit, to take in the space for himself, or walk past your bookcases. When we are seated, the guests need not be provided with food and drink in a murderous tempo. Catching up on news is perhaps more fitting. Just like friendship, the meeting with guests needs to occur in a safe zone, without stress. You do not need to put on airs, neither as host (for example, by preparing a much too complicated meal), nor as guest (for example, by participating "brilliantly" in the conversation from the edge of your chair). The departure and the leaving should likewise occur without haste. Thus, as host you do not suddenly tell your guests that they can still catch the last train, for that is a transition that deserves some attention and time.

At work, there are comparable opportunities to sanctify a little the receiving of visitors or the conversation with colleagues who stop by. I try to make it a habit to lay down some time before the appointment to turn my computer off, to switch off the telephone, so that, with the arrival of my guest, I do not need to turn abruptly from one thing to another. When the guest has arrived, a period of acclimatization is important for him. To get down to business abruptly looks quite unsuitable to me and actually counterproductive. During the conversation a climate of a (calm) meeting should emerge—actually this is the basic meaning of "conversation," which is related to *conversio*. In the conversation it is important that the souls are truly in conversation together, turning to each other, and are not bogged down in matters that lie outside the conversation. That is how a safe zone is created.

Yet another form of hospitality is for guests whom you cannot even see, but those who visit you via telephone or electronic mail. The trick is then to try to be a good porter, for example, by not letting the visitor wait at the gate; by a good word on the telephone in which no rush or stress is conveyed; by careful replying to mail, also electronically; by trying to really accept and understand a message and, if necessary, to pass it on.

These forms of hospitality, like in an abbey, have their limits, demarcations, and a striving for balance. There are periods of availability and periods to be reserved for yourself, so that, on this level, you will be able to turn to others and to get into conversation.

At the monastery cemetery of Saint Willibrord's Abbey, Brother Alouis Canters (frère Louis), who was a porter for decades and died at an advanced age during the exercise of his function, is buried. His fellow brother, the artist Henri Boelaars, designed a beautiful vignette for his tombstone, which expresses in a single image the content of Benedictine hospitality: two hands around a key, above it the word *pax* (peace). The key lies in the peaceful meeting.

7

A Stimulating Training School for the Lord

In the previous part we met a few Benedictine attitudes to which Benedict dedicated separate chapters of his Rule. Additionally, there are several monastic virtues, attitudes directed toward excellence, which did not receive a separate chapter yet illuminate the Rule in several places. A few of them I wish to highlight briefly because they may be exercised and cultivated fruitfully outside the monastery as well.

Discipline and Space

Many people today exert themselves to become or to remain fit. They have particularly physical "fitness" in mind, and a prosperous line of business provides services promoting that need. A spiritual component also belongs to that: how do we remain physically fit and vital so that we can be fruitfully of service? Self-discipline belongs to that, partly in order that we might not be filled with ourselves and what we "bring in" both physically and spiritually, so that we no longer notice the shortcomings of people around us.

The training school Benedict had in mind is characterized by a finely balanced joining of discipline and space. The order of the day, the dealing with food and drink, with work, study, and recreation, the correction of what hurts the person and the community, the process in which novices grow into the community—all this demands a disciplined personal and social life. This discipline is, however, directed to life and space, not to oneself and to the restricting of people. Discipline is a precondition for growing toward a free and joyful life, while a lack of discipline makes people unfree because they remain stuck with habits that block growth.

Moreover, the monastic discipline is to be viewed with sufficient flexibility. In many places in the Rule the abbot is counseled to bear in mind the measure and the power of discernment with the circumstances and the differences among brothers. This power of discernment is indicated in the Rule as *discretio*.

The Capacity for Discernment and Prudence

In chapter 64 about the abbot and his personal qualifications, Benedict calls *discretio* the mother of the virtues (*matris virtutum*). This fits in with an ancient ethic of virtues, which Aristotle gave systematic form. Virtues are acquired attitudes of excellence based on examples and training. Every virtue has to do with an optimal and positive human quality, often in the "middle" of two non-virtues. Thus bravery is an attitude of excellence that lies between the non-virtues of cowardice and foolhardiness. It would, of course, be false to suppose that bravery is a mixture of cowardice and foolhardiness. When you mix two negative and objectionable attitudes, you do not get a positive attitude that is praiseworthy. Excellence is directed to the optimal. But separate virtues such as bravery, justice, strictness, and mercy are attitudes in a limited *domain* of human and social acts that are in their place in limited circumstances and contexts. My father was an excellent butcher, but the qualities that belong to that profession he did not, of course, exercise in conversation with friends or during vacation. Bravery is suitable in battle, but it is not an adequate attitude when you read a story to your children before bedtime. The capacity for judgment, for weighing what the context demands of you, to consider which attitude is suitable and to what measure you keep it, might be called "prudence." It is this prudence that Benedict labels *discretio*.

In the first chapter about the abbot (RB 2) the abbatial *discretio* is firmly emphasized. It consists in the first place in proper conflict management. The abbot must treat monks quite differently in the manner which, at that moment and for that person, is the most suitable. The Netherlands has "the law of equal treatment" (directed to discrimination based on gender and origin). Benedict would gladly agree with this law, for with the acceptance of new monks, differences in status, money, learning, and origin were not allowed to play a role for almost fifteen hundred years. However, concerning the contact between abbot and brothers, the Rule is, in a certain sense, a "law of unequal treatment." Moreover, it is the abbot who must adjust himself to the nature and the comprehension of the brothers, and not the reverse. He needs to adapt, Benedict states, an adapting that proceeds from a hearty willingness to bend to the other who the abbot wants to serve. It will be clear that this needs to be a firm form of adaptability. This is not about blowing with every wind and accepting personal quirks and weaknesses without correction. Otherwise, disintegration arises. The lack of flexibility leads to rigidity in the community, however.

In the chapter on the measure of drink (RB 40), *discretio* of the abbot is again brought up. The proposed daily ration of wine—formulated by Benedict with a certain reserve (also an aspect of discretion), for people differ in their needs relating to eating and drinking—may be deviated from when the work on the land or the summer heat justifies a bit larger ration. This is to be judged by the abbot. With this *discretio*, it is emphasized in this connection that this may be expressed in a realistic view concerning the difference between the ideal (in this case, no wine) and reality (for example, local customs). *Discretio* makes

Benedict and the sensible abbot decide for an achievable and somewhat flexible rule without losing sight of the ideal.

In the chapters relating to correction and punishment of matters that hurt the person of the monk and community life, the abbot is again asked for prudence, the power of discernment, and a certain reserve. For example, he may not, with his own full abbatial weight, demand correction, but have a mature fellow brother possessing sufficient self-knowledge and the talent not to judge too quickly play a mediating role. For, in the context of correction and punishment, knowledge of the heart is required, of the other and of oneself. With this sort of process "the abbot must be aware of his own vulnerability." The awareness of one's own vulnerability and limitations is part of the monastic virtue of humility, the courage to serve. For correction also stands in the sphere of "service," a serving attitude directed to the healing of the person and of the community. Only in the awareness of one's own weaknesses the spiritual father or mother can help and heal, without pride, but with "discretion."

In the chapter on labor and *lectio* (RB 48), discretion is asked from the abbot in the giving of tasks to the weaker and less healthy fellow brothers. With these realities also he needs to deal with care. Such care demands a generous sensitivity for what people can and cannot manage.

In the second chapter on the abbot (RB 64), this is underscored once more. Where it deals with correction it is repeated that this must occur in the right measure. With the assignment of tasks, the abbot must act with so much "feeling for measure" that the weak do not shrink back from tasks that might make them go under, but that something remains to be reached by the strong. One would hope that these verses of the Rule might be displayed in every management office and also that they would be observed.

Correcting What Is Wrong

In a culture in which we often powerlessly or indifferently tolerate one thing or another we know is not right, it may sur-

prise us that Benedict spends so much attention to correction and
sometimes also to punishment of unvirtuous behavior, that is to
say, behavior that is hurtful to the person and the community. We
would not want to copy all forms in use in the late ancient world
without further ado. The fundamental attitude not to "let go" the
wrong, but to straighten it out in a fitting manner, appears valuable
in the long run, however. With Benedict, the correction is always
directed to well-being, even in the rare cases when he advises the
abbot to handle the surgical knife to remove a dangerous spot. The
correction also needs to take place in a sphere of mutual respect
and affection: "the abbot must hate the sin, but love the sinner."
Again, the capacity of discernment is demanded here because the
abbot must be affectionate both to the person and the community.
That is even relevant in what seem to be little things. Abbot Guillaume of Katsberg has made it a habit always to reprimand brothers
who are late for the choral prayers or the common meal, as the Rule
prescribes, simply by inquiring what the reason for their tardiness
might be. He has noted that they mostly indicate valid reasons—a
task that could not be put down, a guest who asked for attention,
the bell being overwhelmed by the noise of a machine—reasons
that explain their tardiness. But Abbot Guillaume tries to make
clear to his brothers that an explication (*explicatio*) is not yet a
justification (*justificatio*). Coming late may be understandable,
but it does injustice to the quality of the mutual choral prayer.
Even small negligences deserve to be corrected because they do
injustice to the *bonum commune*, because they may be inclined to
be somewhat contagious and also to gradually become worse.

Joyful and Durable Frugality

A certain measure of austerity is cultivated in Benedictine life,
but without communal life becoming sour and lean. The abbot
must see to it that the brothers may have at their disposal what
they need. Their nourishment must be sufficient and of sufficient
variety. With the warm meal, Benedict writes, two cooked dishes
must be served, so that those who find the one dish less tasty

may choose the other. On festival days, not only the ecclesiastical high festivals but also important events pertaining to individual brothers and of the community as a whole, an extra effort may be made concerning eating and drinking, and the brothers may enjoy that without embarrassment. The Benedictine attitude contrasts with our culture of overconsumption and permanent superficial pleasure. Yet, in its feeling of measure and variation, it appears to be more durable and genuine.

The same durability is expressed by the dedicated care for everything pertaining to the abbey: buildings, tools, clothing, books, garden, forest, farm, sometimes an abbey school, or a university related to the abbey. Benedict does not like a sloppy waste and a messy life. The well-cared-for physical environment and the well-thought-out arrangement of an abbey exercise the greatest power of attraction to the visitors. The fact that this might work in an infectious manner appeared in the experience of the student referred to above, who, after returning home from a weekend at an abbey, began cleaning up her room.

The respectful dealing with the environment, without dirtying of the area where it is hoped that the facility will remain in use for generations to come, leads to the persuasion of the Benedictine family toward "environmental consciousness" even before this became a generally accepted concept in our culture. A striking number of abbeys, particularly when they are situated in the country, are presently taking initiatives with ecological projects, use of renewable sources of energy, and the training of people, that they might deal respectfully with the environment.

The Association of Benedictine Colleges and Universities[16] has included themes relating to durability and ecology in their curriculum, in addition to courses in which sustainability, peace, justice, globalization, and human dignity are studied in context.

Rest and Patience

The gentleness cultivated in Benedictine manners is pleasantly contrasted with the noisy coarseness that so often characterizes our society. Romano Guardini once described a gentleman as someone without noise. It might be said that Benedict likes to see monastic communities as communities of gentlemen and "gentlewomen" in which people act gently and courteously toward one another because of mutual affection.

Additionally, the climate of quiet patience that characterizes monastic communities if things are well is contrary to the frequently rushed work that targets short-term results, as we meet in so many present contexts. Rest and patience are not synonymous with lethargy and sluggishness. Brother Benet Tvedten says about this: "Though the Benedictine life style is calm and unhurried, there are things which merit immediate attention according to Benedict. What needs to be done, must be done promptly."[17] Benedictine work moves calmly but with determination.

Benedicere: The Good Word, Well Spoken

In an earlier chapter we saw that Benedict is against too much wrong speaking, in which we place ourselves in the center, without offering real space to others, but wishing to outdo others. The appropriate word, spoken in a fitting manner and at the right moment, can be a blessing.

Of course, we all know this in our own personal and social life. In the workplace, the use of words is likewise important. Orders are issued, there is consultation, reports are given, reactions are expressed. What is not expressed might be saying much, however. Listening "with the ear of the heart" is thereby an essential precondition for fruitful living and working. But speaking the right word in the right manner is also essential. In an earlier chapter we saw that the wrong word, or the right word said wrongly, or speaking ill (*male-dicere*) may have serious consequences: internal grumbling (*murmuratio*), further spreading of the poison when leaders speak wrongly and their words have "circulated," causing undesirable spiritual divisions of cells, the formation of spiritual "metastasis" that may be stagnating or lethal. Fortunately, there is also an antidote: the cheerful and well-spoken good word, which may result in a spiritual chemotherapy, but without unpleasant side effects. Bringing "good words" into circulation (*benedicere*) works like balm for the souls in an organization, works by catching on, and results in a positive spiritual divisions of cells. Spite and anger should, of course, be taken seriously as human experiences. If you stick with them, they become "poisonous," however. Spiritual smog, notes Johanna Domek, is something that poisons the breathing of the community. Benedict advises to get rid of this "poison" daily by speaking up, and to be reconciled with your brother before nightfall. Imagine how our community would flourish if this advice of Benedict were taken seriously.

The speaking of a good word demands practice, according to prioress Johanna Domek. It is no different from swimming, cooking well, or beautiful playing of the cello. As we can learn daily to be alert for opportunities to speak a good word, we may also make a habit of reflecting on our daily experiences when we spoke wrongly: in a wrong tone, by insincerity, by emphasizing the negative, or by overlooking the positive.

The right use of the word is an essential part of what we need to learn in the "school of exercise for the Lord," the Lord who shows himself mostly in the face of your fellow sister.

Benedict: The Patron Saint of Humanity and Imperfection

When Brother Benet Tvedten entered Blue Cloud Abbey, he was told that a monastery was a perfect place. After almost half a century of monastic life, the conviction gradually grew in him that Benedict must be the "patron saint of human imperfection." The Rule itself shows that things will go wrong constantly, that brothers will be negligent or get too big for their britches, that differences about power and competence will occur, that quarrels will arise, and so much more that may get derailed in personal and social life. Thus we encounter the attention for correction for what threatens to grow crooked, for an open and hearty ear with the leaders, for reconciliation, for humility, and realism for *conversio* directed to growth. Brother Benet said: "Striving for progress, yes; wanting to reach perfection, no."

Monasteries are not examples of perfection; they are exercise schools in which there is learning and practice even with all fragility. Neither are they places in which one can get a spiritual "free lunch," as it were, without much effort. There is a way to go, but a way with a perspective. It is an attractive way, directed to "good days."

Outsiders can perhaps hardly imagine this, but the acquaintance with this way can evoke a deep longing, as it is beautifully expressed in verse 4 of Psalm 27:

> One thing I asked of the LORD,
>   that will I seek after:
> to live in the house of the LORD,
>   all the days of my life,
> to behold the beauty of the LORD,
>   and look at his face in his temple.

In the film *De grote stilte* [*Into Great Silence*], one of the Carthusians tells us that the monastery had really tempted him and that he fell in love with it. Seeking God together and following Christ attracted him. These seekers of God and followers of Christ chose to live together in an exercise school for the Lord, and indeed, if it is well, it is a very stimulating school where "good days" may be experienced. It is an exercise school that has something to offer people who wish to exercise in a very different context and wish to experience "good days." For oblates and people who are associated with communities of the Benedictine family, that is certainly the case. We wish to bring the Rule of Benedict fruitfully into our own world of home and work, Benedictine spirituality and often the ethos of the community to which we are related, often without explicitly referring to it. But sometimes we also try to pass it on to others, hopefully in a fitting manner.

Notes

[1] The author (of the original Dutch version) used the translation of the *Rule of Saint Benedict* by Frans Vromen, OSB, (1973) because he is most familiar with it. He appreciates also the more recent translation by Vincent Hunink (2000). Leonard J. Doyle has translated *St. Benedict's Rule for Monasteries* by Liturgical Press (1947). In this book, the translator has cited Derkse's quotes in English.

[2] Michael Casey, *Strangers to the City: Reflections on the Beliefs and Values of the Rule of Saint Benedict* (Brewster, MA: Paraclete Press, 2005), 5.

[3] Andrew Nugent, OSB, *The Slow-Release Miracle: A Spirituality for a Lifetime* (Dublin, Ireland: Columba, 2006).

[4] Translated from the original Dutch volume by the title: *The Rule of Benedict for Beginners: Spirituality for Daily Life* (Collegeville, MN: Liturgical Press, 2003).

[5] Unless indicated otherwise, all (unfamiliar) cited place names are located in the Netherlands.

[6] For information on the Carthusians, see www.chartreux.org.

[7] This image is beautifully developed in a lecture by Timothy Radcliffe, OP, during a Congress of Abbots in Rome in 2000, "The Throne of Glory," published in his book *I Call You Friends* (London: Continuum, 2001), 99–113.

[8] The written version of his lecture may be found in: www.let.ru.nl/ V.Hunink/documents/benedictus_nederigheid.htm.

[9] This summary was adapted from Andrew Nugent, OSB, *The Slow-Release Miracle: A Spirituality for a Lifetime* (Dublin, Ireland: Columba, 2006), 86.

[10] "George Steiner: le bonheur d'enseigner," *Le magazine littéraire* (January 2004): 99–103.

[11] Michael Casey, *Strangers to the City. Reflections on the Beliefs and Values of the Rule of Saint Benedict* (Brewster, MA: Paraclete Press, 2008).

[12] A beautiful collection of well-elucidated paintings and photos of reading women is offered by Stefan Bollman, *Frauen die lesen sind gefährlich. Lesende Frauen in Malerei und Fotografie* (München, 2005).

[13] See www.abbaye-pierrequivire.asso.fr.

[14] See www.monasteria.org for information (also about guest quarters) of monasteries of the Benedictine family in the Low Countries.

[15] See www.willibrords-abbey.nl, and www.kasteelslangenburg.nl.

[16] See the general Benedictine website: www.osb.org.

[17] Brother Benet Tvedten, *How to Be a Monastic and Not Leave Your Day Job: An Invitation to Oblate Life* (Brewster, MA: Paraclete Press, 2006).